# Life Kitchen

Recipes to revive the
joy of **taste** & **flavour**

## Ryan Riley

Photography by Clare Winfield    Illustrations by Lara Harwood

BLOOMSBURY PUBLISHING
LONDON · OXFORD · NEW YORK · NEW DELHI · SYDNEY

This book is for you, Mother.

Krista Riley
1965–2013

A special thank you to
Kimberley Duke, my co-founder at Life Kitchen
and my lifelong best friend.

We have loved and lost our mothers to cancer.

Your input on the recipes, the classes and Life Kitchen
overall has helped to make this book and our organisation the
best it can be. I'd also like to dedicate this book to your mother:
this is for you, too, Nicki.

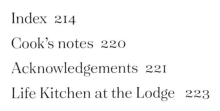

# The Life Kitchen story

I was eighteen years old when my mother Krista was diagnosed with terminal small cell lung cancer. My life changed immeasurably. I became my mother's carer; I spent every day with her, living and breathing her life just as she did. I was a grumpy teenager, the household cleaner and her sofa confidante. Life Kitchen was born of the relationship I had with my mother, our experiences and our pain, and of what we went through as a family during a very difficult time.

In the years that followed my mother's diagnosis, I saw the ups and downs of her life and treatment, from the loss of her hair to the depression, and her fear of dying – a completely reasonable response to her illness, but a shadow cast over her difficult final months. She faced every day with grace and resolve, but there was one thing that hit her particularly painfully: she lost her ability to enjoy food. The barrage of ongoing chemotherapy and radiotherapy took their toll on her sense of taste, dulling flavours and turning food, which she had always loved, into a mere occasional necessity.

At a time when it was so important that my mother found pleasure in food, all the enjoyment and comfort – and even normality – in cooking and eating were gone. In her final months, the only things she could consistently taste were frozen ice pops, mainly for the numbing, cold, sugar hit they offered her.

Two years after her diagnosis, my mother died from her illness. I believe there's only one thing to do with that amount of sadness and pain and that's to turn it into a force for good; find a positive way to reinvent it and somehow give reason to an experience that feels senseless and unfair. Finding the right fit, though, is not easy.

The route to Life Kitchen, like all the best and most rewarding things in life, was not straightforward. After my mother died I was – understandably, I think – feeling a bit self-destructive. One night, probably only a month or so after my mother had died, I found myself in a casino with a friend and not much more than £20 in our pockets. All we wanted was enough money to buy a few drinks. I won £28,000. Of course, at that point I could have taken the money and blown it on a forget-it-all holiday, or tried to turn it into yet more cash at the tables, but it was a turning point. The money enabled me to move with my best friend Kimberley to London. And that's the real start of Life Kitchen, although at the time I didn't know it.

We used the money to pay the rent and we opened a food stall in Camden. I worked in publishing for a small fashion magazine, writing and shooting editorials. And, eventually, I started working as a cookery writer and stylist. In time, I started to think about what it was that I could do to best honour my mother's memory and to make cancer that little bit less painful and unforgiving for those living with it. I thought about my mother's frustration at losing her love of food. Surely this was where my own knowledge and expertise could make a difference.

Of course, what seems a brilliant idea is one thing, but I needed some feedback to see if what was germinating in my imagination was really as innovative as I thought it could be. I took to Twitter: was there a need for a cookery class that would teach people living with cancer all about taste and flavour? Could such a class aim to bring back some of the joy in creating and eating food?

Within a few hours my tweet had gained traction in the form of hundreds of expressions of interest and offers of help. The relationship between flavour and cancer was clearly something that people wanted to talk about. I reached out to the food industry and was overwhelmed when Nigella Lawson and Hugh Fearnley-Whittingstall wanted to support me. *Escape to River Cottage* was my mother's favourite television programme, so where could be more meaningful to launch my first-ever class than at River Cottage itself?

I took that class in February 2018 – and now, some two years later, not only have we held more than 100 free pop-up classes all over the country, encouraging, laughing and learning with so many cancer patients and their families (collectively our guests), but we have also opened our first permanent cookery school at

Mowbray Lodge in Sunderland, my home city. With this book out in the world, too, the reach of Life Kitchen stretches ever further. I couldn't be more proud.

Of course, Life Kitchen isn't just me. First, there's Kimberley – my friend since we were two, my co-founder and my collaborator on the book. Then, there's my family – my sisters and my dad. But Life Kitchen is more than just us, our story and our instinctive attempt at developing recipes to bring a new appreciation of food and flavour to cancer patients. It's a science – and for that, I needed a science expert.

Founder of the Centre for the Study of the Senses at the University of London, Professor Barry Smith is a world authority on taste and flavour, making him the perfect adviser for Life Kitchen. In the six months before I launched my first class, I asked his advice on my recipes (including Carbonara with Mint & Peas on page 156, and Roasted Harissa Salmon with Fennel Salad on page 107 – both now Life Kitchen classics). Barry and I have worked together ever since to identify ingredients, tastes and techniques that can shape the Life Kitchen recipes to make them the most appealing they can be to people who are living with cancer. Our founding principle is simple: to create recipes that have strong, layered flavours, focusing on ingredients rich in umami and trigeminal stimulants (which sounds stranger than it actually is – more about that shortly).

The Life Kitchen family is as rich in knowledge as it is diverse in personal story. It includes not only my friends, family and colleagues who have helped to make it happen, but also our guests and the media and general public who have supported us in more ways than it's possible to recount. Through our free classes and demonstrations, our culinary journey has helped thousands of people whose lives have been affected by treatment for cancer. The privilege of working with our guests has been emotional to say the least – the moments in which we've found a pop of flavour for someone who hasn't been able to taste in a while are some of the most profound of my life.

Something you'll notice throughout the book is that flavour is a far-reaching concept. I've taken ingredients from all over the world and created new dishes, reinvented old classics and perhaps at times thrown things together that may look a little surprising, but (in my opinion) open a whole new world of deliciousness. In itself, that's a Life Kitchen lesson, too – these are our ideas, our flavour profiles, and our recipes created through our knowledge and research, but flavour is very much your own. Use this book as a guide, a form of culinary adventure and inspiration, and never feel constrained by it. I want to inspire you not only to cook the Life Kitchen recipes themselves, but also to turn them into dishes that really work for you.

Go forth and find your flavour.

**Ryan Riley**
Founder

# The recipes, flavours & techniques

Although the dishes in this book are designed for people living with cancer, it is very important to me that the whole family can enjoy them. They are powerfully flavoured, exciting and delicious recipes for everyone. Together, the team at Life Kitchen and I have looked at the science, we've taken advice from people living with cancer and we've used our culinary knowledge to bring the recipes to life – but not every recipe will work for everyone. Living with cancer is an individual experience – there is no single, typical path. Inevitably, then, in writing a book we've had to find breadth and scope in the recipes and hope that most – if not all – of them will appeal to you. It's very important to say that this book is as much yours as it is mine or Life Kitchen's – feel free to adjust any recipe to your own flavour preferences.

That's not to say that we haven't done lots of work in order to bring you recipes that are as tailored to your needs as possible. In order to write the book, we took the recipes out on the road in partnership with Maggie's Cancer Centres. The '#RefineTheRecipeTour' visited nine of the Maggie's centres across the UK to host one-off supper clubs. Overall, more than 100 people tasted over 80 per cent of the recipes in the book. We listened to every piece of feedback we were given and responded in the recipes themselves, refining them every step of the way.

As a recipe writer and cook, I think about how flavours work together in an holistic sense. I consider not only what something tastes like, but also how we respond to it – emotionally and instinctively – when we eat it. I think in terms of punch, zing, brightness, boldness, comfort – and myriad other terms that resonate with me when I think about the effect of a dish on the person eating it. All of those words, though, hide a fundamental science behind our experience of food. The person best suited to describing that science is my science guru, Barry Smith...

# The science of taste & flavour

By Professor Barry C. Smith

My introduction to Life Kitchen came when Ryan called me out of the blue. He wanted to know more about tasting: how it was affected for people undergoing chemotherapy and what could be done to help. His passion was truly inspiring and I was impressed by his intuitive understanding of the idea that we can use ingredients to enhance our experience of flavour. Since that first contact, we have worked together to combine Ryan and Kimberley's cooking flare with the underlying science. To understand how the principles of Life Kitchen work, it helps to spell out the way we taste flavours.

When we eat we usually think that it's our tongue that enables us to pick up all the flavours of food. But it's not. In fact, all that the tongue gives us are the basic tastes: salt, sweet, sour, bitter and umami (savouriness). That's because we have receptors for each of these tastes in our taste buds.

We all know, though, that those tastes are not all our food has to offer. Think of all the foods you could name for their flavour alone: onion, ginger, mango, melon, raspberry, strawberry, lamb, chicken, beef – the list goes on. But, we don't have receptors on our tongue for onion, or mango, or any of the flavours of these foods; our ability to perceive them is not down to our tongues only – rather, it is mostly due to smell.

The sense of smell contributes to tasting flavours – but not in the way we may think. We detect odours by sniffing them

Barry and me in the herb garden at
the Life Kitchen cookery school.

through our nostrils and into our nose. By contrast, we detect flavours as a result of chewing food to release odours that then travel through the mouth to the nose. Odours rise from the oral cavity through the back of the throat to the smell receptors at the bridge of the nose. We chew, then swallow, and, when we swallow, we pulse odours up to the nose to give us that big flavour hit.

In this way, tastes and smells combine to provide our experiences of flavour. But that's not all. The feel of food in our mouths gives us a sense of the creaminess or chewiness, stickiness or crunchiness of a food. This extra dimension – of texture – can make a big difference to how acceptable or desirable foods are to us. Some people don't like their eggs runny, others don't like them firm. Do you prefer your steak served medium or rare? Do you like your tea piping hot or just lukewarm? These decisions are about the touch of what we are eating (or drinking) on the tongue and in the mouth. Texture can add to or detract from our experience of a meal. Think how a chef might add the crunch of pine nuts or al dente vegetables to a creamy, saucy dish to give it interest.

What we think of simply as taste, then, is in fact a combination of the taste, smell and touch of food. And there's more. Think of spicy foods – such as pepper, chilli, horseradish or mustard – which burn a little. That stinging sensation is because these foods irritate trigeminal nerve endings in the mouth and on the tongue. The trigeminal nerve is the fifth cranial nerve that serves the eyes, the nose and the mouth. It springs from just below the ear and branches off into three paths. Stimulating trigeminal nerve endings gives you burning, stinging or cooling sensations from some foods. Think how mustard tastes hot in the mouth, and peppermint cool, even though they are exactly the same temperature. The trigeminal nerve carries temperature and pain receptors. Chemical compounds in spices and herbs can bluff those receptors into feeling heat or coolness even when it's not really there. Your eyes may well up with tears and you may feel pain at the bridge of your nose when you eat too much mustard or wasabi because your brain interprets the signals from the trigeminal nerve as warnings of an attack – your system then floods your eyes with tears to protect them.

What's clear is that taste, smell, touch, temperature and even mild pain can all contribute to our experiences of flavour. And because so many things go on at once, it stands to reason that several things can also go wrong: disruption to any one of these sensory pathways can radically alter our ability to taste food and how much we enjoy it.

At the Life Kitchen classes, those undergoing chemotherapy treatments tell me about the effects on their sense of taste (which we now know is mostly – although not always – in fact owing to a loss of smell). This affects the pleasure people derive from eating. But things are not straightforward. The treatment each person is receiving – including the type and dosages of medication – will affect them in different ways, depending on their illness and how different they were as tasters to begin with.

Ryan and I quickly realised that if smell loss reduces pleasure in food, a good tactic will be to add a little spice or zing and to make a virtue of different textures to make food more interesting. Throughout the book you'll find Taste & Flavour facts to illustrate how ingredients in a particular recipe are working together to enhance your eating experience.

Of course, it's not simply a case of liberally dusting dishes with spices. As well as the individual differences between tasters, there are all sorts of associations at play. For those of us with a working sense of smell, cinnamon is a warm, comforting spice. But to those who can't smell its distinctive aroma, a sprinkle can feel harsh. Menthol or mint may add cooling pleasure, but it is likely to be less agreeable if we can't discern its scent. Think of vanilla. This spice commonly adds sweetness to a dish, even though there is no sugar in it. How so? The effect is because of an association our brain makes between the aroma of vanilla and the sweetness of the foods we usually pair it with – ice cream, chocolate, custard and cake, for example. In the cuisines of cultures that more commonly combine vanilla with fish or salt dishes, vanilla may seem not sweet, but salty.

When it comes to flavours, though, individuality is far more than memories or associations – there are physical considerations to think of, too. Many of the Life Kitchen dishes include a hit of citrus, which provides the sour acidity that livens up food. However, if a side effect of treatment is mouth ulcers, citrus can cause physical pain. In that case, we can omit citrus in any of the dishes and change it for tropical fruits, such as mango or papaya, which have a soothing, creamy texture better suited to those for whom acidity feels too sharp.

And then there is umami. So much of what Ryan does at Life Kitchen is about using umami to enhance our eating experiences. With good reason. Umami is the fifth basic taste, alongside salt, sweet, sour and bitter, and yet many people in the West still haven't heard of it and don't know which foods have it. The Japanese, on the other hand, prize umami and recognise its taste as easily as they recognise saltiness or sourness. Umami is the meatiness you taste in mushrooms, soy sauce and hard cheeses. It also occurs in peas and tomatoes, meat and fish. The taste of umami can boost the other basic tastes, making dishes seem saltier or sweeter without having to add more salt or sugar to them. In this way, umami is a flavour enhancer.

There are two types of umami – glutamates and nucleotides. When we combine foods with these different types of umami, we can produce the tastiest flavours of all. This is called synergistic umami and it's the reason we love so many classic food pairings – cheese and ham, eggs and bacon, tomatoes and anchovies, scallops and pea purée. These are all cases of synergistic umami.

Finally, if you're suffering dry mouth as a result of your treatment, umami-rich foods are known to help. Umami stimulates saliva flow, whetting your appetite and making foods more palatable. In seeking to reignite a love for food or a desire to eat, umami is the most important taste of all.

**Professor Barry C. Smith**
Centre for the Study of the Senses,
University of London

In summary, then, Barry, Kim and I – and the whole Life Kitchen recipe team – make sure that science lies at the heart of our recipe development, focusing on three primary things: acidity, umami and stimulating the trigeminal nerve.

## The role of acidity

Never underestimate acidity – it's a core building block of flavour and we use loads of it in the recipes in the book (and at Life Kitchen in general). Citrus is transformative, adding zing to a dish, pepping it up. That may be because, as Barry explained to me, the tongue's sour receptors fire up more quickly than, say, the sweet receptors (which fire more slowly). The effects are that a little lemon over mushrooms amplifies the bold, earthy flavours; orange zest on roasted vegetables lifts the natural sweetness that opens up as the vegetables caramelise in the oven – and so on.

Wine, tomatoes and vinegar are also ways to add acidity to a dish, and they all pop up in the recipes. (Never more liberally than in the use of red wine vinegar to transform red onions into Pink Pickled Onions – a Life Kitchen flavour hit – on page 78.)

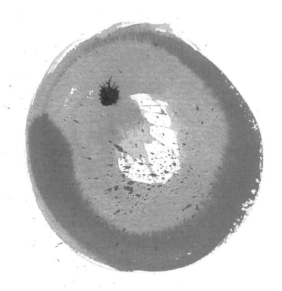

The science of taste & flavour

## The role of umami

At Life Kitchen we like to think of umami as the ladder that sweet, salty, bitter and sour climb to reach flavour town! For this reason, and all the reasons Barry has talked about, we've absolutely packed umami-rich ingredients into our recipes.

Among those ingredients are parmesan, cured meats, tomatoes, peas, mushrooms, soy sauce, potatoes, carrots, fish sauce, shellfish, miso and beetroot (and many others). Each varies in levels of how much umami it contains compared with the others. However, in the recipes we aim to build them together to create more powerful flavour that is known scientifically as synergistic umami, but we like to call it 'super-umami'.

## Stimulating the trigeminal nerve

The main nerve between your eyes, nose and mouth, the trigeminal nerve is responsible for the tingling, almost face-scrunching sensation you get when you eat things like mint, cinnamon, wasabi, mustard and horseradish. We use these stimulants in Life Kitchen recipes to add sensation to your experience of eating the dishes, making it more rounded.

**ABOUT 'FLAVOUR HITS'**
Each chapter in the book opens with two 'flavour hits' – simple recipes that are, in effect, intensely flavoured condiments for you to sprinkle, spoon or drizzle over any of the dishes in the book (or any meal) to add a burst of flavour.

# Key ingredients

There are eleven special ingredients that I really love using in our recipes because of their flavour and versatility. My inner purist wanted to make this list a nice, round ten – but, truly, all of the following culinary gems give food a much-welcome boost and I couldn't bear to leave any one of them behind. The flavour of these ingredients is unmatched elsewhere in the store cupboard and I'm certain that once you have a taste for the decadence of black garlic and brightness of za'atar, and everything else listed over the following pages, they will all become staples in your home, too.

### Black garlic (1)

The bulbs of black garlic are aged over a few weeks and have a sweet, balsamic vibe. Balsajo sells a wonderful black garlic that you can find in local supermarkets.

### Citrus (2)

I think it's fair to say that Life Kitchen relies on citrus – in the form of lemon, lime and orange – as the ultimate ingredient for our food. Lemon, in particular, helps add zing and much-needed acidity to dishes as diverse as the Roasted Onion Soup on page 96 and the Marmite Cheddar Crumpets with Tarragon Mushrooms on page 90, and everything in between. Most of the Life Kitchen desserts heavily feature lemon as a way to cut through the sweetness and reintroduce the pleasure of eating pudding.

### Garam masala (3)

An Indian spice blend that comes in hundreds of different forms, there really is no set recipe for garam masala. The best way to choose which to use is to experiment with different brands and blends until you find one that suits you. To me, a good garam masala includes cinnamon, cardamom, coriander seed, black pepper, cloves, cumin, fenugreek, bay leaf, nutmeg and pimento.

### Maple syrup (4)

One of my favourite ingredients, when we need a bit of sweetness, for me maple syrup just gets the edge over honey – mainly because it's also suitable for vegan diets. Best of all, though, it also contains a superhero aroma molecule called sotolon, which increases the richness and depth of all the other flavours in a dish.

### Nigella seeds (5)

Also known as onion seeds and kalonji seeds, nigella seeds have a mild, sweet-onion flavour, add texture and are a beautiful way to garnish food.

### Parmesan (6)

Also known to the Life Kitchen team as the 'king of cheese', parmesan is immensely umami-rich, making it an excellent ingredient to balance all others (the only suitable replacement for parmesan is a super-strong vintage cheddar). Fundamentally, where there is space for cheese in a recipe, parmesan can fill it.

## Pomegranate molasses (7)

There was a point in recipe development when I couldn't stop adding a drizzle of pomegranate molasses to just about everything. Its tartness is addictive and adds acidity in a way that, I think, no other ingredient can.

## Rose harissa (8)

A North African spice blend, rose harissa consists of roasted red peppers, chilli peppers, garlic and rose petals, usually blended to a paste (which is how we use it at Life Kitchen). Belazu is my favourite brand of rose harissa paste – it is beautifully balanced and perfumed with rose, but not so as you would know it; it also has just the right amount of heat. If you can't find rose harissa paste, though, use regular harissa paste instead.

## Sherry vinegar (9)

Of all the vinegars out there, sherry vinegar wins my heart – and my palate. It's slightly sweet and perfectly mild and is a great substitute for other vinegars if you want to invest in just one type.

## Sumac (10)

Sumac is like the lemon sherbet of the savoury spice world. I can't think of a recipe in this book that wouldn't benefit from a light dusting of sumac.

## Za'atar (11)

This Middle Eastern spice blend has many variations. I like a blend that has sumac, sesame, marjoram and oregano.

# Snacks & Little Bites

I so often hear people in our classes talk about how treatment has quashed their appetite. On top of their altered sense of taste, a lot of our guests seem to be left wondering what to eat when finally a pang of hunger or a need for something (especially something tasty) hits. That's where snacks and little bites come in. In this chapter, you'll find delicious morsels that give a much-needed flavour hit, but in small portions that you can either enjoy immediately or pop in the fridge or cupboard to come back to when you feel like it.

I've borrowed flavours from around the world to give plenty of variety. The Pineapple Tacos with Prawns, Chilli & Lime on page 39, for example, are inspired by a Mexican snack and have plenty of palate-stimulating ingredients: chilli engages the trigeminal nerve (which connects our nose, mouth and eyes and is crucial to our sensory experience of food; see page 20) and boosts our sense of smell; lime adds brightness to the other ingredients. Together, the ingredients rally around to increase saliva production, making the tacos (literally) mouthwatering. This approach – a synergy and chemistry of flavours intended to tempt and excite – is replicated in all the dishes in the chapter, with myriad umami-rich and otherwise flavour-packed ingredients at play.

Two flavour hits open the chapter. The first is Gremolata (see page 34). A powerful, bright and beautiful dressing, this gremolata is for spooning generously over most of the chapter's recipes (there are specific suggestions on the page), but you can also add it to simple scrambled eggs, and any of your favourite salads or fish and meat dishes. The garlic, extra-virgin olive oil, parsley and lemon provide everything from umami to acidity.

The second is Mint Pickled Pomegranate Seeds (see page 37). Lightly pickling pomegranate gives the seeds an extra sharpness that works in particular harmony with fresh mint. Try sprinkling them over the Roasted Broccoli with Chilli Yoghurt & Orange on page 43 to add a wonderful fruitiness. Alternatively, and seeing as cheese and fruit is one of my favourite combinations, try them over the Whole Roasted Feta with Olive & Green Chilli on page 40, which makes just about as perfect a partnership as there can be.

Finally, I want to make a special mention of the Mayonnaise Library on pages 54–5. These flavoured mayonnaises are worth rustling up if you need a quick dip or condiment for anything from a simple sandwich to the Smoky Sweetcorn Cheddar Fritters on page 49. The Classic Mayo adds a decadent, satisfying creaminess – and given a burst of extra flavour can be all you need to give even the simplest snack or meal a new dimension. We've made suggestions for how to use some of the flavoured mayonnaises in the recipes, but feel free to swap things around to suit your own taste buds.

**Flavour hit**

# Gremolata

*An Italian dressing, gremolata brightens up all kinds of meat and fish dishes, but a little sauce like this – whizzed up fresh – is a great way to get in that extra flavour hit to just about anything. Sometimes I like to add a green chilli or some oregano depending on how I'm intending to use it, so feel free to experiment with the herbs and even the spices. You can keep the gremolata in a sterilised jar in the fridge for 2–3 days, but it will lose a little colour in that time, so for that reason it's best to eat it on the day you make it.*

Makes about 120ml

4 garlic cloves

1 lemon, zest and juice

a large handful of parsley, roughly chopped

a pinch of salt

100ml extra-virgin olive oil

Put all the ingredients except the olive oil in a food processor and whizz to combine. With the processor running slowly, add the oil through the feed tube until everything comes together.

If you don't have a food processor, use a pestle to pound the ingredients in a large mortar, then gradually add the oil; or finely chop everything and mix it all together with the oil in a bowl.

***Especially good for spooning over...***
Roasted Broccoli with Chilli Yoghurt & Orange (see page 43)
Smoky Sweetcorn Cheddar Fritters (see page 49)
Grilled Baby Gem Lettuce with Blue Cheese (see page 67)

Snacks & Little Bites

# Mint pickled pomegranate seeds

*We use pomegranate a lot in the Life Kitchen classes. The sour tang of the seeds means that they brighten any dish. Plus, I think there's something deeply satisfying about the way that the mini pockets of juice burst on your tongue and the little red jewels liven up the visual appeal, too. Store the pickled seeds in a sterilised jar in the fridge for up to 1 week.*

Makes about 200g

100g pomegranate seeds

a small handful of mint leaves

100ml red wine vinegar

Place the pomegranate seeds and mint leaves in a clean, heatproof container.

Place a small saucepan on a high heat, add the red wine vinegar and bring it to a rolling boil.

Carefully pour the vinegar over the pomegranate seeds and leave to steep until cool. Transfer to a sterilised jar.

*Especially good for sprinkling over...*
Whole Roasted Feta with Olive & Green Chilli (see page 40)
Roasted Broccoli with Chilli Yoghurt & Orange (see page 43)
Lime Falafels with Curried Mayonnaise (see page 52)
Camembert Potatoes (see page 63)

# Pineapple tacos with prawns, chilli & lime

*My all-time favourite recipe from the Life Kitchen classes, pineapple tacos is the dish that gets the greatest number of emotional reactions from our guests. Once, a wonderful man called Mike – who is 75 years old and hadn't tasted anything in a very long time as a result of his treatment – found this recipe a complete revelation. So many others have said the same thing. Pineapple tacos are a novel idea, but once you've made them, you won't look back.*

Makes about 20 tacos

100g cooked prawns, shelled

1 red or green chilli, finely chopped, plus extra to serve (optional)

1 lime, zest and juice, plus extra wedges for squeezing (optional)

1 spring onion, sliced into rough matchsticks

1 pineapple, peeled and sliced into wafer-thin circles

a small handful of coriander leaves

In a bowl, mix the cooked prawns with the chilli, the lime zest and juice and the spring onion.

Fold each pineapple round in half to resemble a taco shell. Fill each shell with an equal amount of the prawn mixture, sprinkle over a few coriander leaves and squeeze over some extra lime, if you like. Serve immediately with optional extra chilli on the side.

**TASTE & FLAVOUR FACT**
Fresh pineapple contains the enzyme bromelain (lost when the fruit is tinned), which breaks down proteins into amino acids and tenderises meat. In Life Kitchen classes, the most significant feature of fresh pineapples is their power, for some people, to eliminate a metallic taste that can occur as a side effect of their treatments.

# Whole roasted feta with olive & green chilli

*Olives are delicious as they are, but when they're baked in the oven and served with feta cheese, they really come alive. Basil is such a wonderfully aromatic herb, adding a touch of sweetness and balance to savoury, spicy feta. Add the anchovies to give this recipe an extra umami kick, and serve with a lovely, crunchy baguette or on plenty of crackers, or crumbled over a salad.*

Serves 2–4

3 tbsp black olive tapenade

3 green chillies

2 tbsp extra-virgin olive oil

200g feta

a small handful of basil leaves, plus a few extra to garnish (optional)

a couple of tinned anchovies (optional)

Heat the oven to 220°C.

Put the tapenade, chillies and olive oil in a food processor and whizz to a paste.

Lay a double layer of foil on a work surface and place the whole feta in the middle.

Spread the paste over the top and sides of the feta. Lay the basil leaves on top and add the anchovies, if using, on top of the basil. Fold the foil tightly around the feta, leaving no gaps.

Place the foil parcel on a baking tray and bake the wrapped feta for 20 minutes, then remove the parcel from the oven and open it up. Remove the feta from the foil and serve garnished with a few extra basil leaves, if you like.

Snacks & Little Bites

# Roasted broccoli with chilli yoghurt & orange

*Citrus brings life to almost every ingredient it meets, not only lending uplifting aromas, but providing the often much-needed acidity that balances out other flavours. Roasted broccoli pairs deliciously with aromatic orange, but you could equally brighten it with a grating of lemon zest or a squeeze of lime. This dish makes a quick lunch served up with flatbreads, or a tasty side to roasted fish.*

Serves 2

230g long-stem broccoli

olive oil

1 tsp capers

a small handful of flaked almonds

3 tbsp full-fat Greek yoghurt

1 tsp Chilli Oil (see page 80)

1 orange, zested and halved

a sprinkling of sumac

chilli flakes, to serve (optional)

Heat the oven to 180°C.

Place the broccoli on a baking tray and drizzle with olive oil. Spoon the capers over and bake for 15 minutes. Then, sprinkle the flaked almonds over and bake for a further 5 minutes, until the broccoli is tender and the almonds are golden.

While the broccoli is baking, in a bowl combine the yoghurt and chilli oil. Peel and segment one orange half. As soon as the broccoli is ready, squeeze the juice from the remaining orange half over the top, sprinkle with a good dusting of sumac and orange zest and serve with a dollop of the chilli yoghurt (sprinkled with chilli flakes, if you like) and the orange segments on the side.

# Gyoza parcels

*Gyoza are perfect hot pockets of aromatic goodness and actually don't take long to put together. This recipe uses shortcrust pastry instead of gyoza pastry, mainly because it's more readily available, but also because it's easier to mould into delicious morsels. However, if you can get your hands on gyoza pastry, the results will be more authentic and just as perfect. Aromatic ginger is a flavoursome pick-me-up – the powerful smell alone can be an excellent way to stimulate your appetite.*

Makes 12–15 parcels

2 x 320g sheets of ready-rolled shortcrust pastry, at room temperature

**FOR THE FILLING**

400g pork mince, or 400g raw king prawns, shelled

1 large carrot or 2 small carrots, roughly chopped

1/2 leek, roughly chopped

4 spring onions, roughly chopped

2 tsp ginger paste

2 tsp garlic paste, or 4 garlic cloves, chopped

1 tsp toasted sesame oil

2 tsp light soy sauce

1/4 tsp white pepper

1 tsp caster sugar

**FOR THE EGG WASH**

1 egg beaten with 1 tsp milk

1 tsp nigella seeds

**FOR THE GINGER KETCHUP**

6 tbsp tomato ketchup

1 tbsp ginger paste

1/2 tsp toasted sesame oil

Heat the oven to 180°C.

First, prepare the egg wash and ketchup. In a small bowl, mix the egg and milk mixture with the nigella seeds. In a small serving bowl, mix all the ketchup ingredients together to combine. Set both aside.

Put all the filling ingredients in a food processor and whizz to a rough paste. Set aside.

Use a circle cutter the size of a coffee mug (or use a coffee mug) to cut out the pastry into 12–15 rounds.

Add 1–2 teaspoons of filling to the middle of each pastry circle, taking care not to overfill. Brush the edges of the pastry with a little water and fold each circle in half over the filling, pressing the edges together to seal. Brush the parcels with the egg wash, then transfer them to a baking tray and bake for 15–20 minutes, until golden brown and cooked through. Serve with the ginger ketchup alongside for dipping.

# Curried fennel & red onion bhajis

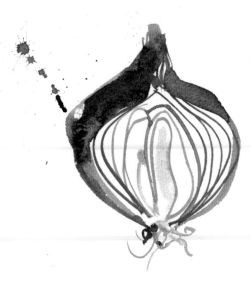

*Is there anything more satisfying than something hot and crispy straight out of the frying pan? Yes, something hot, spiced and crispy with tomato salsa on top! Bhajis are so easy to make – using only one bowl, a grater and a frying pan. The fennel in these bhajis brings a pop of aniseed flavour, which is a wonderful match for the tart and sweet, umami-rich tomatoes. Use chickpea flour rather than plain flour for a gluten-free version, if you prefer.*

Makes 12–16 bhajis

**FOR THE BHAJIS**

1 large fennel bulb

1 large red onion

1 green chilli, finely chopped

1 tsp ground cumin

1 tsp ground coriander

2 tsp garam masala

1 tsp medium curry powder

1 tsp nigella seeds

8 tbsp plain flour

1 or 2 eggs

vegetable or rapeseed oil

a sprinkling of sumac

salt and freshly ground black pepper

**FOR THE SALSA**

6 cherry tomatoes, roughly chopped

a small handful of coriander, roughly chopped

1 lime, zest and juice, plus extra wedges to serve

Roughly grate the fennel and red onion into a bowl and add the green chilli. Add the spices, nigella seeds, flour and 1 egg. Season to taste, then mix well aiming for the consistency of thick pancake batter. If it looks too floury, add the second egg.

Place a frying pan on a medium–high heat and add a generous glug of oil. When hot, cook the bhajis in batches: place 4–6 individual tablespoonfuls of the bhaji mixture in the pan and press them down slightly with a spoon to flatten so that they cook evenly. Once the bhajis are browned on one side (about 2–3 minutes), turn them over and fry for a further 1–2 minutes, to brown the other side. (Take care not to splash yourself with oil when you flip them.) Remove the cooked bhajis from the pan and pop them aside to drain on kitchen paper while you cook the next batch.

(Alternatively, you can use a deep-fat fryer if you have one: heat the oil to 180°C and drop in spoonfuls of the mixture for about 1½ minutes per batch, until browned all over.)

Transfer the cooked bhajis to a serving dish, sprinkle with sumac and keep warm while you make the salsa. Combine the tomatoes and coriander in a serving bowl, then add the lime zest and juice. Serve alongside or on top of the hot bhajis, with extra wedges of lime for squeezing over.

# Smoky sweetcorn cheddar fritters with chipotle mayonnaise

*Chilli is one of my favourite ingredients and there are so many varieties to play around with. Chipotle, a dried jalapeño chilli used often in Mexican cooking, isn't overly spicy, but adds an irresistible smokiness to a dish. These fritters are so easy to whip together. If you don't have all of the ingredients, feel free to experiment: swap out the sweetcorn for garden peas, or the spring onions for red or brown onions, for example.*

Makes 12–16 fritters

**TASTE & FLAVOUR FACT**
Like mustard and horseradish, chilli makes the mouth feel hot with sensations of local, oral burning. However, the tongue isn't being burned. These differences are not because of temperature, but because of irritation of the trigeminal nerve endings (see page 20).

**FOR THE FRITTERS**

1 x 200g tin of sweetcorn

3 tsp chipotle paste

50g vintage cheddar, grated

4 spring onions, finely chopped

a small handful of mint leaves, roughly chopped

70g plain flour

1 or 2 eggs

vegetable or rapeseed oil

**TO SERVE**

Chipotle Mayo (see page 55)

lime wedges (optional)

Combine all the fritter ingredients except the eggs and oil in a large bowl. Break in 1 egg, then mix well aiming for the consistency of pancake batter. If it looks too floury, add the second egg.

Place a frying pan on a medium–high heat and add a generous glug of oil. When hot, cook the fritters in batches: place 4–6 individual tablespoonfuls of the fritter mixture in the pan. Once the fritters are browned on one side (about 1–2 minutes), turn them over and fry for a further 1–2 minutes to brown the other side. (Take care not to splash yourself with oil when you flip them.) Remove the cooked fritters from the pan and pop them aside to drain on kitchen paper while you cook the next batch.

(Alternatively, you can use a deep-fat fryer if you have one: heat the oil to 180°C and drop in spoonfuls of the mixture for about 2–3 minutes per batch, until browned all over.)

Transfer the cooked fritters to a serving dish and serve with the chipotle mayo for dipping and lime wedges for squeezing over, if you like. (The mayo will keep in the fridge for a couple of days, if you don't use it all.)

# Pea fritters with preserved lemon mayonnaise

*Peas are (perhaps surprisingly) packed full of umami. The tiny green spheres contain just about the same amount of glutamates (see page 23) as garlic. These fritters are served with preserved lemon mayonnaise. Preserved lemons are a traditional Middle Eastern ingredient that provide an extra zing that's hard to get from regular lemons. One jar of preserved lemons will last you about 1 month if you store them in the fridge, so they are well worth seeking out.*

Makes 12–16 fritters

**FOR THE FRITTERS**

1 shallot

a small handful of mint leaves

a small handful of dill

2 preserved lemons, or the zest and juice of 1 lemon

1 green chilli

300g frozen peas

2 tbsp malt vinegar

100g plain flour

1 or 2 eggs

vegetable or rapeseed oil

**TO SERVE**

flaky salt

Preserved Lemon Mayo (see page 55)

lemon wedges

Chop the shallot, mint leaves, dill, preserved lemons and green chilli as small as you can and put them in a large bowl, or pulse them together in a food processor and transfer the mixture to the bowl.

Add all the other fritter ingredients, except the eggs and the oil, to the bowl and use your hands to fully combine. Add 1 egg and mix, breaking up the peas and squashing them slightly until you have a thick batter. If the mixture is too floury, add the second egg.

Place a frying pan on a medium–high heat and add a generous glug of oil. When hot, cook the fritters in batches: place 4–6 individual tablespoonfuls of the fritter mixture in the pan. Once the fritters are browned on one side (about 1–2 minutes), turn them over and fry for a further 1–2 minutes, to brown the other side. (Take care not to splash yourself with oil when you flip them.) Remove the cooked fritters from the pan and pop them aside to drain on kitchen paper while you cook the next batch.

(Alternatively, you can use a deep-fat fryer if you have one: heat the oil to 180°C and drop in spoonfuls of the mixture for about 1½ minutes per batch, until browned all over.)

Transfer the cooked fritters to a serving dish. Sprinkle with flaky salt and serve with the preserved lemon mayonnaise alongside for dipping, and with wedges of lemon for squeezing over. (The mayo will keep in the fridge for a couple of days, if you don't use it all.)

# Lime falafels with curried mayonnaise

The strong, tangy flavours of these lime falafels give them good punch all on their own, but the curried mayonnaise, which is super-simple to put together, adds great balance for the herbs and spices. Alternatively, you could choose any of the mayos from the Mayonnaise Library on pages 54–5, if you prefer.

Makes about 24 falafels

**FOR THE FALAFELS**

100g couscous

100ml boiling water

2 tbsp mint sauce

1 x 400g tin of chickpeas, drained

a small handful of parsley

a small handful of mint

a small handful of dill

a small handful of coriander

1 tsp garam masala

1 tsp ground coriander

½ lime, zest and juice

1 tsp nigella seeds

½ green chilli (optional)

1 small egg

vegetable or rapeseed oil

salt and black pepper

**TO SERVE**

warmed flatbreads

Curried Mayo (see page 55)

Pink Pickled Onions (optional; see page 78)

Mint Pickled Pomegranate Seeds (see page 37)

Place the couscous in a bowl, pour over the boiling water and stir through the mint sauce. Cover with cling film and leave for 10 minutes, until the water has been absorbed and the grains are tender.

Meanwhile, place the chickpeas in a food processor with the herbs, spices, lime zest and juice, nigella seeds, chilli, if using, and egg and blend until almost smooth. Add the couscous mixture, season, and blend again. Roll into 24 individual small balls (each just smaller than a golf ball).

For the best results, heat the oil in a deep-fat fryer to 180°C and add the balls a few at time, frying for 4–6 minutes, until golden all over. If you don't have a deep-fat fryer, place a medium saucepan on a high heat and add a generous glug of oil. Slightly flatten your falafels to give them a better cooking surface for the pan. When the oil is hot, fry in batches (about 4–6 at a time) for about 1–2 minutes, or until the falafels are deeply browned on one side. Then, flip them over and fry for another 1–2 minutes to brown the other side. Pop each batch aside to drain on kitchen paper while you fry the next.

Serve on warmed flatbreads with the curried mayonnaise, and some pink pickled onions and mint pickled pomegranate seeds, if you like.

# Mayonnaise library

*Used as a dip or dressing, a simple, flavoured mayonnaise can add interest that will transform a dish. Start with the Classic Mayo (see below), then choose your variation and stir through the ingredients (or whizz them if they need breaking down). If you don't have time to make your own classic mayonnaise, a good-quality, shop-bought version can work just as well as a base for the other flavours.*

## For the Classic Mayo (1)

Makes 1 small jar

4 egg yolks

1 tbsp good-quality extra-virgin olive oil

150ml rapeseed oil

1 tsp white wine vinegar

salt

Use an electric hand whisk or food processor to whisk the yolks well, add a drizzle of the olive oil and continue to whisk. Very slowly, add the remaining olive oil and all the rapeseed oil. Keep whisking continuously, to make sure the oil and the yolks don't split. After about 2–3 minutes, the mixture should begin to thicken. Keep whisking and add the vinegar, then finally season with salt to taste. Transfer to a sterilised jar and store in the fridge for up to 1 week.

## For the variations

### CHIPOTLE MAYO (2)

6 tbsp Classic Mayo

zest of 1 lime

about 1 tsp chipotle paste, to taste

### GREMOLATA MAYO (3)

6 tbsp Classic Mayo

1 tbsp Gremolata (see page 34)

### PRESERVED LEMON MAYO (4)

6 tbsp Classic Mayo (or natural yoghurt)

1 preserved lemon, diced small, or the zest and juice of 2 lemons

### ROCKET & CAPER MAYO (5)

8 tbsp Classic Mayo

a small handful rocket, finely chopped

2 tsp capers, chopped

### LIME MAYO (6)

8 tbsp Classic Mayo

2 limes, zest and juice

### BLACK GARLIC MAYO (7)

8 tbsp Classic Mayo

4 black garlic cloves, crushed or finely chopped

1 tsp sherry vinegar

### ROASTED GARLIC MAYO (8)

12 tbsp Classic Mayo

half a bulb of roasted garlic, flesh squeezed from the skin

### HARISSA MAYO (9)

6 tbsp Classic Mayo

1 tbsp rose harissa paste

### CURRIED MAYO (10)

6 tbsp Classic Mayo

2 tbsp mild curry powder

6  7

8  9

10

# Goat's cheese & beetroot croquettes

*Beetroot and goat's cheese is a well-known pairing (and for good reason), but it's actually the maple syrup (a Life Kitchen key ingredient; see page 28), chilli and chive dressing that makes these croquettes special. You'll need a goat's cheese with a soft rind and chalky centre for the best results with this recipe.*

Makes about 10 croquettes

**TASTE & FLAVOUR FACT**
Maple syrup provides sweetness but also richness and depth of flavour. This is because maple syrup contains significant levels of sotolon, a powerful aroma molecule that at higher concentrations has the scent of fenugreek and curry.

**FOR THE CROQUETTES**

150g soft goat's cheese

1 whole cooked beetroot (about 75g; vacuum-packed is best), diced very small and patted dry with kitchen paper

1 egg beaten with 1 tsp milk

50g panko breadcrumbs

vegetable or rapeseed oil

freshly ground black pepper

a few small mint leaves, to serve (optional)

**FOR THE DRESSING**

5 tbsp maple syrup

1 red chilli, finely chopped

a small handful of chives, finely chopped

Mash the goat's cheese in a bowl using a fork. Add the beetroot and mix well (I like to use my hands) until everything comes together, then season liberally with black pepper. Break off small pieces of the mixture and roll each piece between your palms into a ball about the size of a sprout, and set aside.

Place the egg and milk mixture and the breadcrumbs in separate bowls. Dip the goat's cheese and beetroot balls into the egg and milk mixture, then into the breadcrumbs, turning them to coat fully. Once all the balls are coated, pop them in the freezer for 15 minutes, to firm up.

Meanwhile, mix together all the dressing ingredients in a bowl and set aside.

Place a frying pan on a medium–high heat and add a generous glug of oil. When hot, add the croquettes 5 at a time, turning them until golden all over (about 2 minutes). Pop them aside to drain on kitchen paper while you fry the next batch.

Once all the croquettes are cooked, place them in a serving dish and either pour over the dressing, or serve it alongside for dipping. Scatter the croquettes with a few small mint leaves, if you like.

Snacks & Little Bites

# Spiced kale crisps

*Trust me when I say that the use of kale here is not about being healthy – it is strictly about flavour and texture. This recipe takes about 15 minutes to prepare and is so worth it! The texture of roasted kale resembles a classic crisp, with all its comforting familiarity. If you like, play around with some different spices – for example, chipotle would work well with the paprika.*

Makes about 5 handfuls

½ tsp ground cumin

½ tsp smoked paprika

¼ tsp ground cinnamon

¼ tsp chilli powder

½ tsp olive oil

100g curly kale leaves

zest of 1 lemon

½ tsp golden caster sugar

¼ tsp salt

Heat the oven to 180°C.

Combine the spices and the oil in a large bowl. Add the kale and mix well, making sure the leaves are well coated.

Shake off any excess oil from the leaves and place them on a baking tray. Spread them out in a single layer to ensure every leaf reaches its maximum crispiness. Pop the tray in the oven for 10 minutes, until the leaves are crisp but not browned.

While the kale is baking, combine the lemon zest, sugar and salt in a bowl. When the kale is ready, remove from the oven and sprinkle with the lemon mixture. Serve immediately.

Snacks & Little Bites

# Camembert potatoes

*In the world of umami, parmesan is the king of cheese, but camembert, with its own fair share of glutamates, definitely earns its place as a crown prince. Potatoes are another umami source, so putting the two together provides my personal favourite when it comes to flavour synergy. This dish of crispy cheese, tangy pickles and fluffy potatoes makes the perfect side to any dinner – but, equally, it's an ideal cosy lunch. Choose a camembert that is nice and firm, and not too ripe.*

Serves 3

1 whole camembert (250g)

about 30 new potatoes

1 tsp salt

olive oil

10 large pickled onions, quartered, plus 3 tsp of the pickling vinegar

a few thyme sprigs, leaves picked

Heat the oven to 180°C.

Slice the whole camembert horizontally into 3 rounds. Set aside.

Put the potatoes in a large pan of salted water on a high heat. Bring them to the boil and cook for about 20 minutes, until soft. Drain, then divide the potatoes between three individual ovenproof serving dishes (or use one large ovenproof dish, if you prefer). Sprinkle with the salt, then drizzle over some olive oil.

Pop the camembert rounds on top of the potatoes, scatter in the pickled onions and thyme and bake for 15–20 minutes, until the cheese turns molten and bubbling, and is golden and starting to crisp at the edges. Remove from the oven and drizzle over the pickling vinegar for an extra flavour hit. Serve immediately.

# Cucumber & carrot pickle salad

*Pickles are an easy way to pack flavour into a meal. This lively pickle salad works especially well with the addition of the mint. In the dressing, sherry vinegar gives a sweet acidity, while soy slips in a little umami and nigella seeds add texture. The salad is delicious alone when you want something sharp and fresh, but works equally happily as a side to fish or rice.*

Serves 2–4

1 cucumber, sliced into ribbons

2 large mixed-colour carrots, sliced into ribbons

a small handful of mint leaves

**FOR THE DRESSING**

4 tbsp sherry vinegar

3 tbsp light soy sauce

1 tsp chilli flakes

1 tsp nigella seeds

Place the sliced vegetables in a large serving bowl. In a separate small bowl, combine the dressing ingredients.

Pour the dressing over the vegetables and scrunch everything together well with your hands. (This gets the flavours into the vegetables.) Tear the mint leaves over the top, and serve immediately.

**TASTE & FLAVOUR FACT**
Pickling transforms foods into sharp, textured treats for the mouth. The crunchy texture occurs because the pickling liquid removes water from the vegetables and the acid environment stiffens the structure of their cell walls to give them bite and crunch.

# Grilled baby gem lettuce with blue cheese

*The laziest salad in the land is this grilled gem. Warming the lettuce is unusual, but achieves something special: a salad that is comforting, as well as fresh. At Life Kitchen, we do a lot of drizzling citrus over something hot – the heat somehow intensifies the effects of the juice. In this case, the citrus (lemon) adds its signature freshness and really transforms the flavour of the humble lettuce, giving it some zing. Blue cheese adds umami.*

Serves 1–2

2 heads of gem lettuce, quartered

1 lemon

a sprinkling of smoked sea salt (or regular sea salt, if you can't find smoked)

50g blue cheese, such as stilton

a sprinkling of sumac, to serve (optional)

Place a dry frying pan on a medium heat. When hot, add the lettuce quarters and cook on one side for about 2 minutes, then turn them over and cook for a further 2 minutes, until browned all over. (Do this in batches, if necessary.)

Once the lettuce has browned, zest the lemon over the pan, then cut it in half and squeeze in the juice from both halves over the top (catch the pips in your fingers).

Remove the pan from the heat and transfer the lettuce to a serving plate. Sprinkle with salt, then crumble over the blue cheese. Sprinkle with sumac to serve, if you like.

# Gem lettuce with strawberry, mint & balsamic dressing

*Vinegar introduces powerful flavour into food. Strawberries and balsamic vinegar work especially well together, because the sharp sweetness of the balsamic enhances the flavour of the fruit. For an extra hit of umami, you could add a handful of cherry tomatoes, too. If you want to go further, a handful of olives and a few anchovies would elevate this salad from a humble side to a flavour-packed main. A topping of roasted hazelnuts or almonds would also work well.*

Serves 2

2 heads of gem lettuce

a handful of parmesan shavings (optional)

**FOR THE DRESSING**

8 strawberries

a handful of mint leaves

4 tbsp balsamic vinegar

First, make the dressing. Place all the dressing ingredients in a blender and pulse until smooth and combined. (Alternatively, chop the strawberries, then use a fork to lightly mash them together with the mint and vinegar.)

Separate the gem lettuce leaves into a serving bowl. Spoon the dressing over the top and scatter over the parmesan shavings, if using, to finish.

**TASTE & FLAVOUR FACT**
Strawberry's complex aroma shares some of the same scent molecules that we find in peach, balsamic vinegar, caramel, nutmeg, cut grass and basil. This overlap in aromas is why the strawberry pairs so well with the balsamic vinegar in this recipe.

# Ice lollies

*When my mother was ill, the only thing that brought her a little bit of pleasure was ice lollies. For the book, I've created a few different ice lollies with punchy flavours that deliver that welcome refreshing hit. If you have an ice-cream machine, these recipes work really brilliantly as sorbets: simply put the cooled mixture in the fridge for 1 hour, then transfer it to the machine and churn until you reach the desired consistency, then freeze.*

*Each makes about 12 ice lollies*

## Rhubarb & cardamom

300g rhubarb, diced

1 tsp vanilla bean paste

150g granulated sugar

10 cardamom pods, cracked slightly with the side of a knife

a pinch of salt

Put all the ingredients in a large saucepan with 350ml of water and place it on a high heat. Bring to the boil, then reduce the heat so that the mixture simmers for 20 minutes, or until the rhubarb has completely fallen apart. Strain the liquid through a sieve into a bowl and discard the pulp. Allow the liquid to cool completely, then pour it into reuseable ice-lolly moulds. Pop the moulds in the freezer for about 4–6 hours, until solid.

### Pineapple & mint

300ml pineapple juice

300g pineapple, peeled, cored and diced

2 tbsp maple syrup

a handful of mint leaves

Put all the ingredients in a blender and blitz until smooth. Strain the liquid through a sieve into a bowl and discard the pulp. Pour the liquid into reuseable ice-lolly moulds. Pop the moulds in the freezer for about 4–6 hours, until solid.

### Honeydew melon & rose water

1 whole honeydew melon, peeled, deseeded and flesh diced

300ml whole milk

100ml double cream

180g golden caster sugar

3 tsp rose water, or more to taste, if you like

Put all the ingredients except the rose water in a large saucepan on a high heat. Bring to the boil, then reduce the heat and simmer for 20 minutes, until the melon is soft. Tip the mixture into a blender, or use a hand-held stick blender, and blitz until totally smooth. Strain the liquid through a sieve into a bowl and discard the pulp. Add the rose water to the strained liquid and mix well. Allow the liquid to cool completely, then pour it into reuseable ice-lolly moulds. Pop the moulds in the freezer for about 4–6 hours, until solid.

### Raspberry & tomato

10 cherry tomatoes

a large handful of raspberries

120g granulated sugar

1 tbsp maple syrup (optional)

Put all the ingredients in a saucepan with 300ml of water and place on a high heat. Bring to the boil, then reduce the heat and simmer for 15 minutes, until the tomatoes and raspberries are soft and the sugar has dissolved. Strain the liquid through a sieve into a bowl and discard the pulp. Allow the liquid to cool completely, then pour it into reuseable ice-lolly moulds. Pop the moulds in the freezer for about 4–6 hours, until solid.

# Quick & Easy

There were times during my mother's treatment when she was really low on energy, when having some tasty, quick and easy recipes to cook up and eat would have been especially helpful for her. I've written this chapter with that memory of my mother very much in mind. Flavour isn't necessarily time-consuming – often, it's just about finding ingredients that will combine beautifully, then bringing them together and letting them do the work on their own.

The Orzotto on page 113 is a perfect example, and is among my favourite recipes in the book. It's a simple pasta dish with a gorgeously vibrant rose harissa (see page 29) and goat's cheese sauce. There are only three basic ingredients in that sauce, but they collaborate to have an impact far greater than the sum of their parts: lemon provides acidity to stimulate the palate; goat's cheese brings umami; and the spices in the harissa stimulate the trigeminal nerve to set alight the senses, while the rose activates the sense of smell. Once you have a key dish like this and you also know what ingredients have properties that will stimulate your own palate, you can begin to experiment – adding your own twists to personalise a recipe to suit you.

At Life Kitchen, we're such fans of rose harissa that it pops up several times in the recipes throughout the book. This is not only because rose harissa is a powerful source of flavour, but also because once you've bought a jar, it's good to have lots of ideas for how to use it in different and exciting ways (like in this chapter's Life Kitchen classic: Roasted Harissa Salmon with Fennel Salad, on page 107).

Pink Pickled Onions (see page 78) are our signature flavour hit at Life Kitchen and the first flavour hit in this chapter. These bright pink treasures are quick to make, versatile to use and gorgeous to look at. During our classes, I often talk about the importance of taking that extra minute to plate up food in a pleasing way. To say that eating begins with the eyes is a cliché, but it's true. We've given suggestions for how to use them sprinkled over some of the recipes in this chapter, but don't let us limit you – even a humble cheese toastie is brought to life with a splash of their shocking pink.

The second flavour hit is our homemade Chilli Oil (see page 80). It combines two varieties of chilli so that when you use it, the oil will provide smokiness with a base layer of spicy heat. Again, we've given you suggestions for some especially good pairings, but feel free to experiment: drizzle or spoon the oil over your favourite foods for an instant, fiery hit, or try it stirred into yoghurt, then spooned over a dish for a more mellow chilli flavour.

**Flavour hit**
# Pink pickled onions

*These little cerise beauties can add oomph to anything. They keep very well, so on days when you don't really feel like doing much, add them to just about any dish to bring a pop of vibrancy and flavour – see below for some recommended pairings in this chapter. Try adding a couple of cardamom or coriander seeds to the pickling liquid for a little something extra, if you like. Or, some chopped mint or a whole green chilli works well, too. The onions will store in a sterilised, airtight jar in the fridge for about 7 days.*

Makes about 500g

4 red onions, thinly sliced into half moons

150ml red wine vinegar

a pinch of salt

Place the onions in a medium bowl. Pour over the red wine vinegar and season with the salt. Leave the onions to steep in the liquid for at least 15 minutes, until they take on a vibrant pink hue. Transfer the onions and the pickling liquid to a sterilised jar and seal with a lid.

***Especially good for spooning over…***
Marmite Cream-cheese Toast with Mushrooms (see page 84)
Satay Greens (see page 100)
Roasted Harissa Salmon with Fennel Salad (see page 107)
Jacket Potatoes with Black Garlic, Spring Onion & Feta (see page 116)
Mango & Halloumi Salad (see page 121)

**Flavour hit**

# Chilli oil

*If you don't already have one, a jar of chilli oil should be a staple in your home. You can make this one very easily (it will keep for about 7–10 days in a sealed, sterilised bottle in the fridge). Chipotle chillies are dried, smoked jalapeños and have great depth of flavour; the red chilli flakes add an intense, fragrant heat. If chipotle isn't your favourite dried chilli, though, you could try others – for example, guajillo will give a sweeter, milder flavour, while pasilla has smokiness, fire and sweetness all rolled into one.*

Makes 200ml

200ml rapeseed oil

40g dried chipotle chilli flakes

20g red chilli flakes

Place a saucepan on a medium heat and add the oil. Bring it to a simmer – be very careful, as the oil will be extremely hot. After a few moments, drop in a chilli flake: if the oil is hot enough, the flake will sizzle slightly. Remove the pan from the heat and stir in both types of chilli flake. Set aside and allow to cool completely.

Pour the cooled chilli oil into a sterilised jar and seal with a lid.

*Especially good for drizzling over...*
Marmite Cream-cheese Toast with Mushrooms (see page 84)
Spiced Sweet Potato with Tomato Jam & Yoghurt (see page 88)
Curried Mackerel Noodles (see page 108)
Papaya Salad (see page 123)

# Ploughman's toastie

*One of the best examples of super-umami is the humble cheese-and-ham sandwich – a reassuring combination that is the perfect palate-booster. Here, I've borrowed a few elements from an old-school Ploughman's Lunch and popped them between bread to create a modern, easy-going twist on a well-loved classic.*

Serves 1

2 tbsp unsalted butter

2 slices of any white bread you like

30g vintage cheddar, grated

2 slices of thick-cut ham

4 strong pickled onions, sliced

2 tbsp brown sauce

Use half the butter to butter both bread slices on one side. Layer the cheese, ham and onions on top of one of the buttered slices, then top with the second slice, buttered-side downwards. Spread the exposed sides of the bread (the top and bottom of the sandwich, turning the whole thing over carefully) with the brown sauce.

Place a frying pan on a medium heat. Add the remaining butter and allow it to melt. Carefully add the sandwich to the pan and fry gently for about 3 minutes on each side, until deliciously toasted all over.

Quick & Easy

# Marmite cream-cheese toast with mushrooms

*Eggs are a very good way to pack lots of amino acids (which the body needs to build proteins) into your breakfast, while Marmite and mushrooms work together to offer a powerful, super-umami flavour hit. This toast makes an easy, warming breakfast, or a lunch or light dinner.*

Serves 1

4 tsp full-fat cream cheese

½ tbsp Marmite

boiling water, from a kettle

1 egg

olive oil

1 large mushroom, thinly sliced

1 lemon, zest and juice

1 slice of any bread you like (seeded sourdough is a favourite)

a sprinkling of sumac, to serve (optional)

Mix together the cream cheese and Marmite in a small bowl.

Place a small saucepan on a high heat and add the boiling water. Allow the water to start bubbling again, then carefully add the egg. Reduce the heat so that the water comes to a gentle rolling boil, and cook the egg for 6–7 minutes – this should give you the perfect soft-boiled egg. Remove from the water using a slotted spoon and set aside.

Meanwhile, place a frying pan on a medium–high heat and add a generous glug of oil. When hot, add the mushroom and fry for about 5–6 minutes, until crispy and dark. Sprinkle in the lemon zest and juice and set aside.

Shell and halve the egg. Toast the bread to your liking and spread over the Marmite cream cheese. Spoon the mushroom on top and add the halves of soft-boiled egg. Sprinkle with sumac, if you like.

Quick & Easy

# Hot & cold pickled tomatoes with chilli yoghurt

*Pickled tomatoes. What a revelation. The sweet tanginess of the vinegar really pairs well with the savouriness of the tomatoes, creating something beautifully balanced. Chilli yoghurt helps the tomatoes to sing, and brings the whole dish a light-handed freshness (there is no end to the list of ingredients you can mix into yoghurt to make it exciting). The pickled tomatoes will keep for 2–3 days in the fridge in a sealed container.*

Serves 3–5

150ml red wine vinegar

¼ tsp fennel seeds

6 coriander seeds

2 bay leaves

12 mixed-colour cherry tomatoes, halved or quartered

2 tbsp full-fat Greek yoghurt

1 tsp Chilli Oil (see page 80)

**TO SERVE**

warmed flatbreads or naan breads

a small handful of mint leaves

Stir together the vinegar, both seeds and the bay leaves in a bowl. Place a saucepan on a high heat and pour in half the liquid (with half the aromatics). Bring to the boil, then turn off the heat. Divide the tomatoes between two bowls and pour the hot liquid into one bowl and the cold into the other. Leave for 5 minutes.

Meanwhile, combine the yoghurt and chilli oil in a bowl.

To serve, spread the warmed breads with the chilli yoghurt, top with both hot and cold tomatoes (discarding the bay) and scatter over the mint.

# Spiced sweet potato with tomato jam & yoghurt

*Its spicy earthiness makes fresh jalapeño my chilli of choice for this dish, although chipotle paste (made from dried jalapeños) would work as well. The yoghurt provides creaminess and the roasted sweet potato brings all the textures and flavours together. Tomato jam is a great addition not only to this dish, but also to toasties, salads and grilled fish.*

Serves 2

1 sweet potato, cut into wedges

2 shallots, halved or quartered lengthways

olive oil

1 tbsp smoked paprika

1 lemon, zest and juice

salt and freshly ground black pepper

150g full-fat Greek yoghurt, to serve

### FOR THE TOMATO JAM

1 tsp vegetable or rapeseed oil

1 shallot, sliced into rings

12 cherry tomatoes, halved

1 green jalapeño, sliced

1 tsp medium curry powder

1 tsp golden caster sugar

1 tsp sherry vinegar

Heat the oven to 180°C.

Lay the sweet potato and shallot wedges on a baking tray, drizzle well with oil and season well with salt and pepper. Roast for 20 minutes, then remove from the oven and sprinkle over the smoked paprika. Toss the vegetables around to stop them sticking and cook for about a further 10 minutes, until the potatoes are roasted and soft.

While the potatoes and shallots are cooking, make the tomato jam. Place a frying pan on a medium–high heat and add the oil. When hot, add the shallot rings and cook for about 2 minutes, then add the halved tomatoes and the jalapeño slices. Leave everything to soften for about 4 minutes, then add the curry powder and golden caster sugar and mix well. After 1 minute, add the sherry vinegar and a dash of water to bring everything together, then remove the pan from the heat.

Transfer the potatoes and shallots to a serving plate, drizzle over the lemon juice and add a scattering of lemon zest, then serve with the yoghurt (add a little zest to this, too, if you like) and the tomato jam alongside for dipping.

Quick & Easy

# Marmite cheddar crumpets with tarragon mushrooms

*They say that Marmite is one of those ingredients that either you love or you hate, but I'm a middle-grounder. I love the way it adds richness to cheese dishes, for example – in this recipe its bold flavours offset the saltiness of the cheddar (and the creaminess of the butter) on the crumpet. Umami is boosted in the form of mushrooms, with the tarragon adding an unmistakable aniseed note for extra punch.*

Serves 2

2 crumpets

unsalted butter, for spreading and frying

1 tsp Marmite

olive oil

20g vintage cheddar, grated

6 chestnut mushrooms, sliced

a few tarragon sprigs

1 tsp maple syrup

1 lemon, zest and juice

salt and freshly ground black pepper

Toast the crumpets to your liking, then spread them equally with butter and then Marmite. Set aside.

Place a frying pan on a medium heat and add a glug of oil. When hot, add the cheddar in two little piles, keeping each pile in a rough crumpet-sized circle. Place one crumpet on top of each cheesy circle, Marmite-side downwards, and fry for about 2 minutes, until the cheese is melted, golden and crunchy. Invert the crumpets on to a plate, placing them cheese-side upwards, then set aside.

Using the same frying pan, add the mushrooms with a little butter and a drop more oil. Fry on a high heat for about 5–6 minutes, until the mushrooms take on plenty of colour. Add the tarragon and cook for 1 minute, then add the maple syrup and the lemon zest and juice, and turn to coat everything evenly. Remove from the heat.

Place one crumpet on a second plate. Top both crumpets with equal amounts of the mushroom and tarragon mixture, then season to taste and serve immediately.

**TASTE & FLAVOUR FACT**
Marmite is full of umami. When the nucleotides in Marmite are combined with the glutamates in mushrooms and cheddar we have synergistic umami (see page 23) that boosts the combined flavour.

Quick & Easy

# Baked camembert prawns with chilli

*This recipe features some classic flavour pairings: prawns with garlic, basil with tomatoes, and even soy with basil (Thai-style). Although you might not expect to see all those combinations together in one recipe, they work so deliciously together that this cheesy treat is definitely greater than the sum of its parts.*

Serves 2

10 raw prawns, shelled

1 red chilli, finely chopped

10 sun-dried tomatoes

1 tbsp garlic paste

a small handful of basil leaves, roughly chopped

1 whole camembert (250g), sliced horizontally in half

crusty white baguette, to serve

**FOR THE DRIZZLE**

1 tbsp light soy sauce

1 tbsp balsamic vinegar

Heat the oven to 200°C.

In a bowl, mix together the prawns, chilli, tomatoes, garlic and basil. Pop the mixture on top of one camembert half. Place the other half on top (to make a sort of prawn sandwich), then transfer to a round baking dish or on to a baking tray. Bake for 25 minutes, until the camembert is oozy and the prawns are cooked through.

While the camembert is baking, mix together the drizzle ingredients in a small bowl.

To serve, spread the cheese on hunks of bread and add the drizzle, or simply lace the baked camembert with the drizzle and help yourselves.

# Harissa aubergine & flatbreads

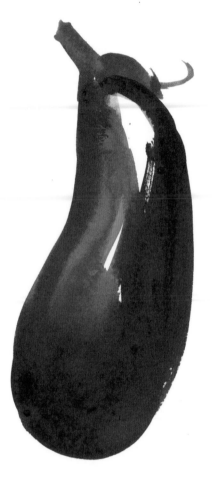

*Aubergines are one of my favourite flavour carriers. Cooked as they are here, they become deliciously caramelised, and the soft flesh soaks up all the flavours of the other ingredients. Rose harissa, a key ingredient (see page 29) in the Life Kitchen cupboards, lends spiced, perfume-like notes, transforming the aubergine into something that feels truly decadent. Serve with flatbreads for an easy snack, but you could serve it with rice for a more substantial meal.*

Serves 2

4 tbsp rapeseed oil

1 large aubergine, diced

4 tbsp rose harissa paste

2 tbsp sherry vinegar

2 tbsp maple syrup or honey

1 lemon, zest and juice

1 tbsp za'atar

salt and freshly ground black pepper

**TO SERVE**

warmed flatbreads

a few mint leaves

Mint Pickled Pomegranate Seeds (see page 37)

Place a large saucepan on a high heat and add the oil. When hot, add the aubergine dice, season with a generous sprinkle of salt and pepper, then fry, turning carefully, for about 10 minutes, until the aubergine is soft on the inside and browned and crispy on the outside. Then, add the harissa, vinegar, syrup or honey, and lemon zest and juice and mix well. Sprinkle the za'atar over the top. Serve on warm, fluffy flatbreads with a few scattered mint leaves and pomegranate seeds.

# Roasted onion soup

*This bowl of soup is full of complex flavours, but is just so simple to put together – it is one of those soups that warms you both literally and figuratively with its reassuring sense of comfort. Roasting vegetables is an excellent way to boost their natural sweetness and also one of the easiest ways to build flavour into soups. The butter adds a smooth silkiness. I like to have my bowlful served with plenty of seeded bread.*

Serves 2–3

4 large onions, halved

vegetable or rapeseed oil

a couple of thyme sprigs

a couple of rosemary sprigs

½ red chilli

2 tbsp light soy sauce

50g parmesan or vintage cheddar, grated

25g unsalted butter

1 lemon, zest and juice

500ml hot vegetable stock

salt and freshly ground black pepper

**TO SERVE**

2–3 tbsp full-fat Greek yoghurt

chilli flakes (optional)

Heat the oven to 180°C.

Put the onion halves, cut-side downwards, in an ovenproof dish with a generous glug of oil. Throw in the thyme, rosemary and chilli. Season everything well with salt and pepper, then roast for about 35 minutes, or until the onions are deeply golden and caramelised.

Remove the dish from the oven and tip the contents into a blender with the soy sauce, cheese, butter and lemon zest and juice. Add the hot vegetable stock a little at a time, blitzing between each addition, until you reach your preferred consistency.

Return the soup to the pan and bring it to the boil so that it's piping hot. Ladle the hot soup into individual bowls, swirl in a little yoghurt, and sprinkle over a few chilli flakes, if you like.

Quick & Easy

# Sticky gochujang cauliflower

*Gochujang is a spicy, Korean red-pepper paste, and in this recipe gives the sauce a delicious flavour. Comforting Korean fried chicken is the inspiration, but the Life Kitchen version comes with cauliflower rather than meat. The roasted cauliflower's crispy little dimples and bumps catch all of the sweet, sticky, spicy sauce for an easy – but irresistible – light bite. (This dish is really good with fluffy rice or warmed flatbreads to make it more substantial.)*

Serves 2

1 cauliflower, separated into florets

olive oil

salt and freshly ground black pepper

### FOR THE SAUCE

4 tbsp gochujang

4 tbsp maple syrup

2 tbsp light soy sauce

4 tbsp rice vinegar (white wine vinegar or sherry vinegar would work, too)

1 lemon, zest and juice

### TO SERVE

1 tsp nigella seeds

¼ tsp sesame oil

lemon wedges (optional)

Heat the oven to 240°C.

Place the cauliflower florets on a baking tray and rub them with a little salt and pepper and olive oil. Roast for about 25 minutes, or until the florets have taken on a golden hue.

Towards the end of the cooking time, put all the sauce ingredients, along with 6 tablespoons of water, in a saucepan on a medium heat. Bring the mixture to the boil, then reduce the heat and allow to simmer for 2–3 minutes, until the sauce is bubbling and thickened. Remove from the heat and set aside.

Once the cauliflower florets are beautifully golden, add them to the pan with the sauce, tossing to coat generously. Transfer to a serving dish, sprinkle over the nigella seeds and sesame oil and serve with lemon wedges on the side for squeezing over.

# Satay greens

*These spring greens go from sidekick for a Sunday roast to satay supernova in no time. I guarantee you will want to make this easy dish for dinner multiple times a week. Prawns would make a good addition for a non-veggie version – add them just after the mushrooms and be sure to cook them through.*

Serves 2

a handful of cashew nuts

1 tbsp crunchy peanut butter

2 tbsp light soy sauce

1 lime, zest and juice

½ red chilli

½ green chilli

½ tsp caster sugar

2 garlic cloves, chopped

1 tsp ginger paste

½ tbsp cornflour

vegetable or rapeseed oil

10 shiitake mushrooms or 2 large portobello mushrooms, thinly sliced

1 head of spring greens, thinly sliced

Heat the oven to 180°C.

Scatter the nuts on to a baking tray in a single layer and roast for 6–8 minutes, until toasted.

Place the toasted nuts with everything except the oil, mushrooms and spring greens in a blender or food processor and blitz to form a sauce. Set aside.

Place a frying pan or a wok on a high heat and add a drizzle of oil. When hot, add the mushrooms and fry for about 4–6 minutes, until nicely coloured. Add the spring greens, moving them around all the time so that nothing burns.

Once the greens are wilted (about 2–3 minutes), add the sauce to the pan or wok and sauté for about 2–3 minutes, until all the vegetables are nicely glazed.

Serve immediately on its own or with some jasmine rice.

Quick & Easy

# Marmite courgettes

While this recipe looks extremely simple (and it is), it really brings a massive hit of our good friend umami. Both soy and Marmite are deep and rich in flavour, and the courgettes act as a wonderful flavour carrier without being overpowering. The maple syrup brings a touch of sweetness, and a sprinkling of fragrant za'atar adds herby, citrus notes that perfectly complement the lemon. I like to serve this with the Romesco on the following pages, alongside a fluffy flatbread or with some steamed rice.

Serves 2–4 with the Romesco (see page 105)

a small handful of hazelnuts

2 tbsp dark soy sauce

2 tsp Marmite

2 tsp maple syrup

4 courgettes, halved lengthways

1 lemon, zest and juice

a sprinkling of za'atar (optional)

Heat the oven to 200°C.

Scatter the nuts on to a baking tray and roast for 4–6 minutes, until lightly toasted. Remove from the oven and when cool enough to handle, crush them using the back of a spoon or the end of a rolling pin. Set aside.

In a bowl, combine the soy sauce, Marmite, and maple syrup. Using a sharp knife, score the cut sides of the courgettes in a criss-cross pattern and cut the scored courgette lengths in half.

Using a pastry brush, brush the cut sides with the Marmite and soy mixture and place the courgettes, cut-sides upwards, on a baking tray. Bake for 35–40 minutes, until tender, sticky, and crispy at the edges. Sprinkle over the hazelnuts, the lemon zest and juice and the za'atar (if using) while still hot.

Quick & Easy

# Romesco

We've barely changed this classic Romesco recipe – it's so good it really needs very little help at all. Roasted red peppers are sweet and juicy and a perfect partner for hazelnuts or almonds. The vinegar's acidity gives an additional lift. Serve the Romesco with bread, or for an extra-rich and accidentally vegan dinner, pair it with the Marmite Courgettes (see page 102).

Serves 2–4

150g hazelnuts or almonds

2 large roasted red peppers from a jar

2 large garlic cloves

a small handful of parsley

2 tbsp tinned chopped tomatoes (optional)

2 tsp sherry vinegar

1 tsp cracked black pepper

3 tbsp olive oil

1 tsp maple syrup

salt and freshly ground black pepper

Heat the oven to 180°C.

Scatter the nuts on to a baking tray in a single layer and roast for 6–8 minutes, until toasted.

Reserving a few whole toasted nuts, throw everything, except the seasoning, in a food processor or blender and pulse until you have a smooth, textured sauce. (If you don't have a processor or blender, chop everything as small as you possibly can and combine it in a big bowl.) Season to taste and serve scattered with the reserved whole nuts.

# Roasted harissa salmon with fennel salad

*One of the first recipes I wrote for our Life Kitchen classes, this roasted salmon takes about 15 minutes from start to finish and is a certain crowd-pleaser (it has even converted my chilli-phobic dad). Rose harissa (see page 29) is a perfect balance of smoky, hot, fresh and slightly sweet. For a veggie version, use cauliflower instead of salmon: roast the cauliflower with some oil, salt and pepper until golden (about 25 minutes), then slather over some harissa and finish it for 5 minutes back in the oven.*

Serves 2

**TASTE & FLAVOUR FACT**
When we cook fish (or meat) at a high temperature, we trigger the Maillard reaction. This begins with the chemical reaction between the amino acids and the sugars in the food, which browns the surface and produces delicious roasted flavours and aromas as it cooks the flesh from the outside in.

2 tbsp rose harissa paste

1 tbsp olive oil

2 wild salmon fillets (about 120g each)

1 fennel bulb, sliced into matchsticks, fronds reserved

3 tbsp full-fat Greek yoghurt

1 lime, zest and juice

1 tsp nigella seeds

**TO SERVE**

extra-virgin olive oil

lemon wedges (optional)

Heat the oven to 180°C.

Mix together the harissa and oil, then use a pastry brush or teaspoon to coat the salmon fillets generously with the mixture. Place the salmon in a baking tray and roast for about 8 minutes – it's ready when the flesh flakes when pressed with the back of a spoon.

Meanwhile, put the fennel matchsticks in a bowl with the yoghurt, lime zest and juice and most of the nigella seeds. Toss to combine.

Place a salmon fillet on each plate with a serving of the fennel salad alongside. Scatter over the reserved fennel fronds and the remaining nigella seeds. Serve drizzled with olive oil, and with lemon wedges on the side, if you like.

# Curried mackerel noodles

*My friend Iftekar introduced me to curried mackerel – he makes a stunning mackerel bhuna that I knew I had to use in some way. This is my quick, comforting and cheap version and a good excuse to use that tin of mackerel that's probably been sitting at the back of the cupboard for some time. The mint and butter give this dish a fresh, glossy flourish to finish it off.*

Serves 2

¼ tsp salt, plus 2 tsp for cooking the noodles

2 x 125g tins of mackerel in oil, drained, oil reserved

1 large onion, finely chopped

3 large garlic cloves, finely chopped

1 red chilli, finely chopped

1 tsp ground cumin

1 tsp garam masala

1 tsp ground turmeric

¼ tsp freshly ground black pepper

375g dried egg noodles

1 tbsp unsalted butter

a handful of mint leaves

1 tbsp Chilli Oil (see page 80)

Put the 2 teaspoons of salt in a large saucepan of water and bring to the boil.

Place a large frying pan on a medium heat and add a little of the mackerel oil (discard the rest of the oil). When hot, add the onion and sauté for 8–10 minutes, until lightly caramelised.

Add the garlic and chilli, reduce the heat to low, and fry for about 5 minutes, until the garlic is softened.

Add the cumin, garam masala, turmeric and ¼ teaspoons of salt and pepper, gently stir to combine, then after about 1 minute, add a splash of water and roughly flake in the mackerel.

Put the noodles in the boiling water and stir once. Cook according to the packet instructions, then drain and stir them into the pan with the mackerel. Stir in the butter and scatter over the mint. Finally, spoon over the chilli oil and serve immediately.

# Roasted garlic cacio e pepe

*The classic cacio e pepe is a simple combination of cheese, pepper and pasta – which I think covers all the main food groups in just three ingredients and means there's not much you have to do to give the flavours a boost. Traditionally, Italians make this dish using pecorino cheese, but I've switched it out for parmesan, which has more umami richness. Roasting the garlic brings out its hidden, mellow sweetness.*

Serves 2–4

1 small garlic bulb

2 tbsp tricolor (black, red and green) peppercorns, finely ground or bashed in a mortar

25g unsalted butter

2 tsp salt, plus extra to season

400g dried pasta (campanelle, farfalle, penne or spaghetti work well)

100g parmesan, grated, plus extra to serve

freshly ground black pepper

Heat the oven to 180°C.

Wrap the garlic bulb tightly in foil and place it on a baking tray. Roast for 25–30 minutes, until soft. Set aside to cool a little, then squeeze the cloves to release the garlic paste into a bowl.

Put a saucepan of water on to boil, then start the sauce. Place a frying pan on a medium heat and add the ground peppercorns, toasting lightly for 2–3 minutes to release the aromas and give a deeper flavour to the final sauce. Add the butter and allow to melt, then stir through the roasted garlic paste to combine. Leave on the lowest heat.

Put the 2 teaspoons of salt in the pan of boiling water, then cook the pasta according to the packet instructions. A couple of minutes before the pasta is ready, remove 2 large mugfuls of the starchy pasta water and gradually stir them into the sauce. Allow the sauce to bubble away until reduced by half (about 4–6 minutes).

Meanwhile, reserve another cup of pasta water and then drain the pasta in a colander.

Once the sauce has reduced, add the parmesan and stir until melted – at this point the consistency should be silky and thick and the sauce should be beige and speckled with toasted peppercorns.

Mix the drained pasta into the sauce until fully coated. If it all looks too dry, gradually add the reserved pasta water and stir again over a low heat to warm through. Season to taste, sprinkle over a little extra grated parmesan and serve immediately.

# Orzotto

When pasta cooks it releases starch into the water, which is why, when you're making a pasta with a simple sauce, it's always good to add a bit of the pasta water towards the end of cooking – it gives your sauce a glossy look and silky texture. I've used rose harissa paste in this recipe to create a punchy, bold flavour with a mild heat. Once the goat's cheese goes in, there emerges a tangy, creamy and moreish sauce. If you can't find orzo, you can use any other pasta you like. I love this dish as it is, but it would be great served up with some smoked fish or crusty bread on the side, too.

Serves 2–3

2 tsp salt

250g orzo

150g soft goat's cheese, plus extra to serve

2 tsp rose harissa paste

1 lemon, zest and juice

a small handful of chives, finely chopped

1 tsp nigella seeds

Put a large saucepan of water on a medium heat, add the salt and bring to the boil. Add the orzo and boil for 6–8 minutes, or according to the packet instructions, until tender.

Once the pasta is almost ready, in a separate saucepan, melt the goat's cheese with its skin on (it has tons of flavour, so don't be tempted to remove it). Add the harissa and lemon juice, then a couple of spoonfuls of pasta cooking water.

Once the pasta is ready, reserve a cup of pasta cooking water, then drain the orzo. Tip it into the pan with the sauce and turn to coat. If it looks a bit dry, gradually add the reserved pasta water, as necessary, and stir well. Stir through the chives, lemon zest and nigella seeds, crumble over a little extra goat's cheese and serve immediately.

# Red pepper & prawn pasta

*This makes for a simple, but delicious supper on any night of the week. Bucatini are long, hollow versions of spaghetti – the hole down the centre catches extra sauce. The red peppers in this dish have a distinctive, sweet flavour that creates a particularly tasty base sauce when paired with chilli and garlic. I've used prawns, but you could swap them out for crab meat or any other seafood.*

Serves 2

2 red peppers, deseeded, or 3 roasted red peppers from a jar

1 green chilli

3 large garlic cloves

rapeseed oil

1 tsp fennel seeds

a generous pinch of salt, plus 2 tsp for cooking the pasta

100g raw prawns, shelled

250g bucatini

50ml double cream

a large handful of parsley, finely chopped

In a food processor, whizz the peppers, chilli and garlic together until you have fine dice. (Alternatively, finely chop as small as you can.)

Tip the mixture into a saucepan with a generous glug of oil and add the fennel seeds. Sprinkle in the generous pinch of salt and place on a medium heat. Cook, stirring occasionally, for 15 minutes, until the red peppers begin to soften (or until everything is heated through if you're using jarred peppers).

Add the prawns and cook for a further 4 minutes, or until they are pink and cooked through. Keep the sauce warm while you cook the pasta.

Place a large saucepan of water on a high heat, add the 2 teaspoons of salt and bring to the boil. Add the bucatini and cook according to the packet instructions, until tender. Drain, reserving half a cup of the cooking water.

Pour the cream into the sauce and stir thoroughly to combine. Stir through the parsley, then add the pasta, stirring to coat. If the sauce is dry, add a couple of tablespoonfuls of the reserved cooking water to loosen. Serve immediately.

# Jacket potatoes with black garlic, spring onion & feta

*I was brought up on jacket potatoes stuffed with bacon and cheddar. My mother made them for every family event. When she was ill, she'd still gather the strength to rustle them up for us, but never really got to enjoy them herself. So, I devised this recipe for her. Black garlic is an incredible ingredient and worth seeking out: full of balsamic flavours and more mellow than regular garlic, it is unlike anything else. Scale up the recipe to feed a crowd.*

Serves 2

2 baking potatoes

olive oil, plus extra to serve (optional)

50g feta, plus extra to serve (optional)

6 black garlic cloves, chopped

60g unsalted butter

2 spring onions, thinly sliced, plus extra to serve (optional)

1 green chilli, finely chopped

a handful of coriander, chopped, plus a few extra leaves to serve

salt and freshly ground black pepper

chilli flakes, to serve (optional)

Heat the oven to 180°C.

Pierce the potatoes all over and rub them with a little oil. Season the skins with salt and pepper, then bake for about 45 minutes to 1 hour, until the skins are crispy and the flesh is tender. (To save time, you can start the potatoes in the microwave for 8 minutes on full power, then bake them for 20–25 minutes.)

Halve the cooked potatoes and scoop out the flesh into a bowl, reserving the 'jackets'. Crumble the feta into the bowl with the potato flesh, then add all the remaining ingredients, except the seasoning. Using a fork, mash everything together until speckled black and white with the garlic and feta and completely combined, then season to taste.

Spoon the mixture back into the potato jackets, pressing it down with a fork to leave ridges in the top that give a satisfyingly crunchy texture when baked. Pop the potatoes back in the oven for 10 minutes, until warmed through and crispy.

Finish with a sprinkling of crumbled feta, coriander leaves, chilli flakes and spring onions and a drizzle of oil, if you like.

Quick & Easy

# Giant kachumber salad with mango & radicchio

*Inspired by the classic and truly excellent Indian kachumber salad, this version stands up brilliantly on its own, but it also works particularly well as a side to a curry. For the Life Kitchen version, we've supersized it and stepped up the acidity.*

Serves 2

1 red onion, finely sliced

1 lime, zest and juice, plus extra wedges to serve

1 cucumber, halved lengthways

2 large green chillies, sliced

2 large tomatoes, cut into 8 wedges

1 head of radicchio, leaves separated

a small handful of coriander, roughly chopped

1 mango, destoned and sliced

1 tbsp nigella seeds

a handful of mint leaves

Put the onion in a bowl and sprinkle over the lime juice to pickle it lightly.

Using a teaspoon, scrape out the seeds from the middle of the cucumber (add the seeds to iced water with lemon for a refreshing drink, if you like), then slice the cucumber into half moons. Put the cucumber slices in a salad bowl.

Add the sliced chilli to the bowl with the cucumber, followed by the tomato wedges and then the radicchio leaves.

Now add the red onion (leaving any pickling liquid in the bowl), then the lime zest and chopped coriander and toss everything well to combine.

Add the mango slices, sprinkle with the nigella seeds and scatter over the mint leaves. Serve with lime wedges.

# Mango & halloumi salad

*Mango, much like pineapple, wakes up your palate. The lime, maple syrup and sesame oil in the dressing mean that this salad combines zing, sweetness and umami. Altogether, this recipe is (quite literally) mouth-wateringly delicious.*

Serves 2

225g halloumi, cut into 8 slices

80g raw, unsalted peanuts

1/2 mango or 4 slices of pre-cut mango, diced

1 large red pepper, deseeded and thinly sliced

1 shallot, sliced into rings

1/2 cucumber, sliced into ribbons

mint or coriander leaves, to garnish (optional)

**FOR THE DRESSING**

3 limes, zest and juice

2 tbsp sherry vinegar

1/4 tsp sesame oil

2 tbsp light soy sauce

1/2 tsp Chilli Oil (see page 80)

2 tbsp maple syrup or golden caster sugar

Place a dry frying pan on a medium heat. When hot, add the halloumi slices and fry on each side for about 1–2 minutes, until golden. Remove the cheese from the pan and set aside.

Leave the pan on the heat and add the peanuts. Reduce the heat and toast the peanuts gently for about 2–3 minutes, until browned, making sure to move them constantly to prevent burning. Once toasted, remove them from the pan. When they are cool enough to handle, crush them with the back of a spoon or the end of a rolling pin. Set aside.

Put the mango, red pepper, shallot and cucumber in a serving bowl.

In a separate bowl, combine the ingredients for the dressing, then pour this over the mango mixture and turn to coat.

Sprinkle on the toasted peanuts, then top with the hot halloumi and finish with a few mint or coriander leaves, if you like.

# Papaya salad

*For even the most desensitised of palates, this salad has it all: the synergistic umami comes from the soy, tomatoes and fish sauce (which itself can provide a savouriness that is unmatched in other ingredients), sweetness comes from the maple syrup, and the papaya stimulates saliva production to wake up the taste buds. You'll need a slightly underripe papaya to get the best out of this dish – try to find one that is mostly green, but speckled with yellow and orange.*

Serves 2–4

**TASTE & FLAVOUR FACT**
Papaya stimulates saliva production (which helps with dry mouth), and contains similar protein-digesting enzymes to pineapple (see page 39). It is also low in acid and good for those who wish to cut out citrus fruit.

a small handful of raw, unsalted peanuts

1 slightly underripe papaya, peeled, deseeded and sliced into matchsticks

1 shallot, sliced into rings

a handful of cherry tomatoes, halved

**FOR THE DRESSING**

1 tbsp fish sauce

1 tbsp tamarind concentrate

1 tbsp light soy sauce

1 lime, zest and juice

2 tsp maple syrup

a handful of Thai basil leaves, torn

1cm piece of ginger root, peeled and grated

1 green chilli, chopped

Heat the oven to 180°C.

Spread out the peanuts in a single layer on a baking tray, then roast for 6–8 minutes, until toasted. When they are cool enough to handle, crush them with the back of a spoon or the end of a rolling pin. Set aside.

Place the papaya in a serving bowl with the shallot rings and cherry tomatoes and stir gently to combine.

In a separate bowl, combine all the dressing ingredients.

Allow the dressing to sit for 5 minutes to allow the flavours to mingle.

Pour the dressing over the salad, toss everything together and allow the salad to sit for 1 minute, before topping with the crushed peanuts and then serving immediately.

# Cavolo nero with chilli & lemon

*Cavolo nero is my favourite variety of kale – it's a little bolder than the curly variety. In this recipe those deeper undertones are given a balancing lift from the lemon and chilli. Delicious on its own, this is also a great side dish to any meal, but particularly to fish or steak, and it works especially well as a breakfast side with fried eggs and za'atar.*

Serves 2

200g cavolo nero

2 tbsp olive oil

1 red chilli, finely chopped

1 lemon, zest and juice

salt and freshly ground black pepper

a sprinkling of sumac, to serve (optional)

Remove the stalk from the middle of the cavolo nero. Separate the leaves from the smaller stalks, and roughly chop both the leaves and the tender stalks, keeping them in separate piles.

Place a frying pan on a medium heat and add the oil. When hot, add the chilli and chopped stalks. Fry gently for 1½ minutes, then add the chopped leaves and sauté for about 3 minutes, until the leaves have wilted and the stalks are cooked through. Season to taste.

Next, add the lemon zest and juice (be careful as the juice will sizzle and spit when it hits the pan) and fry gently for a further 1 minute. Serve immediately, sprinkled with sumac, if you like.

Quick & Easy

# Roasted tomato & basil mashed potatoes

*In this recipe beautifully creamy mashed potatoes meet slightly sweet and tart tomatoes, rounded off with fragrant basil. I could eat this by the bowlful just on its own, but it is also the perfect side to roasted chicken or fish.*

Serves 2–4

2 tsp salt, plus extra to season

3 potatoes (such as Maris Piper or King Edward), roughly chopped

2 large tomatoes, sliced

vegetable or rapeseed oil

60g unsalted butter, diced

a handful of basil, chopped

freshly ground black pepper

Heat the oven to 220°C.

Put the salt and potatoes in a large saucepan and pour in enough cold water to cover. Place on a high heat and bring to the boil. Cook for about 20 minutes, until the potatoes are soft when pierced with the point of a knife.

While the potatoes are cooking, place the sliced tomatoes on a baking tray. Drizzle with a little oil, season with salt and pepper, then roast for about 15 minutes, until they take on a little colour.

Once the potatoes are cooked, drain them and tip them back into the pan. Add the butter, basil and roasted tomatoes. Season to taste, then mash the mixture together until the potato is smooth. Serve immediately.

Quick & Easy

# Friends
# &
# Family

The recipes in this chapter are intended to be cooked for you and then shared with your nearest and dearest – whether that's a significant other or a gathering of family and friends. Whoever is home for tea, put your feet up, choose a dish and pass the book over to the person who is in charge of the cooking. Of course, that's not to say the recipes aren't great for cooking for yourself, too. If you're feeling up to it, there are also some simpler family lunches and dinners that taste delicious and can't fail to impress (I'm looking at you Parmesan Cod with Salt & Vinegar Cucumber, on page 180).

This chapter is packed with traditional family favourites that have been given the very special Life Kitchen spin. The Masala Tomato Soup with Cheese & Green Chilli Toasts on page 146, for example, retains all the comfort of a classic tomato soup, but we've ramped it up a few notches with plenty of spice and heat.

Can we even talk about eating with family and friends without thinking about lasagne? Our Cardamom & Garam Masala Roasted Lasagne on page 159 is as reassuringly soothing as its Italian predecessor, but this Life Kitchen version is packed out with Eastern flavours. Best of all, roasting the mince and vegetables with the spices in the oven means you're not chained to the hob stirring sauces. That frees up time to chat with those around you, and helps you to conserve energy that you might otherwise expend slaving over the proverbial hot stove.

This chapter's first flavour hit is Umami Crumbs on page 132 and is one of the flavour hits I make the most at home. You can sprinkle the crumbs on just about anything and they will give texture as well as flavour. Their intensity comes from the dried shiitake mushrooms – one of the highest sources of umami in any food – paired with yet more umami from the mighty king of cheese, parmesan (see page 28). The result is one of the most powerful forms of super-umami we use in our recipes.

The Green Chutney (see page 134), the second flavour hit, is a beautiful Indian condiment that has, in my opinion, the perfect balance. It is spicy from the jalapeño, rich from the yoghurt, tangy from the lemon and refreshing from the ginger, and it has a little sugar to give it sweetness. Given that there is a lot of southeast Asian influence in this chapter, it seems the perfect companion for so many of the dishes – although feel free to use it however and as often as you wish.

## Flavour hit
# Umami crumbs

*Packed with flavour, umami crumbs are perfect for sprinkling over salads and pasta, and as a topping for fish and meat. The intense, super-umami comes from the combination of shiitake mushrooms and parmesan cheese and the flavours are lifted by the slight tang of garlic. The crumbs will keep for 1 week in an airtight container, stored in a cool, dark place.*

Makes about 150g

20g dried shiitake mushrooms

20g parmesan, grated

1 tsp garlic granules

100g dried breadcrumbs

In a food processor, pulse all of the ingredients until you have a fine crumb.

Place a frying pan on a medium–high heat. When hot, add the crumbs and dry fry for 2–3 minutes, keeping the mixture moving all the time, until crispy. Then, remove from the heat and allow to cool completely before transferring to an airtight container.

*Especially good for sprinkling over...*
Roasted Cauliflower Cheese (see page 142)
Carbonara with Mint & Peas (see page 156)
Cardamom & Garam Masala Roasted Lasagne (see page 159)
Currywurst Traybake (see page 164)

**TASTE & FLAVOUR FACT**
Shiitake mushrooms are one of the few vegan-friendly ingredients that offer flavour-enhancing synergistic umami (see page 23). This is because they contain both glutamates and nucleotides (in this case the nucleotide guanosine, which acts in the same way as inosinate in meat and fish).

**Flavour hit**

# Green chutney

*Green chutney is one of many wonderful and versatile condiments, but this is one of my favourites because it pairs so well with so many things and is super-simple to make. Not only is it good for spooning over curries and tarts, it also makes a delicious marinade for chicken. This flavour hit is best used immediately – it provides a fiery kick with zesty freshness.*

Makes about 100g

a large handful of mint leaves, roughly chopped

a large handful of coriander (leaves and stalks), roughly chopped

1 green jalapeño, roughly chopped

2cm piece of ginger root, peeled and roughly chopped

1 tbsp garam masala

½ tbsp caster sugar

4 tbsp full-fat Greek yoghurt, plus extra if needed

1 lemon, zest and juice

salt

Put all the ingredients, except the salt, in a food processor or blender and whizz until smooth. Taste and, if the texture is too coarse, add a little more yoghurt until smooth. Season with salt to taste.

***Especially good for spooning over...***
Masala Tomato Soup with Cheese & Green Chilli Toasts (see page 146)
Sprout & Garam Masala Tart (see page 148)
Cardamom & Garam Masala Roasted Lasagne (see page 159)
One-pot Chicken & Rice (see page 170)
Papaya Bhuna (see page 172)
Cauliflower Korma (see page 174)

Friends & Family

# Fennel seed & smoked paprika baked eggs

*From shakshuka to huevos rancheros, it seems that every world cuisine has a version of baked eggs. This is the Life Kitchen version. In this recipe, cooking down the onion and chillies together at the start intensifies the flavours and gives the dish a deeply savoury base. The tomatoes add that umami hit and gremolata brings the vibrancy. Cook the dish in a pan that you can use both on the hob and in the oven to save on the cleaning up. If you don't have one, though, start in a pan and transfer the sauce to an ovenproof dish for baking.*

Serves 2–3

1 onion, very roughly chopped

4 garlic cloves

2 green chillies, roughly chopped

a large pinch of salt, plus extra to season

olive oil

1 tsp fennel seeds

1 tsp smoked paprika

a small glass of red wine (optional)

2 x 400g tins of chopped tomatoes

6 eggs

Gremolata (see page 34)

a sprinkling of sumac

freshly ground black pepper

hunks of good-quality bread, to serve

In a processor, pulse together the onion, garlic and chillies with the large pinch of salt, until finely diced. (If you prefer, dice the ingredients as small as possible by hand, then stir the salt through them.)

Place a lidded frying pan on a low heat and add a little olive oil. When hot, add the diced ingredients, put the lid on the pan (or cover with foil if you don't have a lid) and cook for about 15 minutes, or until you have a golden, fragrant paste. It's very important for the onion to sweeten and to have almost melted away – you may need a little longer than 15 minutes, but if you're still going at 20 minutes, turn up the heat a little.

Meanwhile, heat the oven to 180°C.

Add the fennel seeds and smoked paprika to the pan and fry gently for 2 minutes (lid off), then add the wine, if using. Reduce the sauce for 5 minutes, then add the tomatoes and simmer for 10 minutes, until the mixture is thick enough to hold its shape briefly when pressed with the back of a spoon. If you're using a separate oven dish, transfer the mixture now.

Make 6 wells in the mixture with the back of a spoon and crack 1 egg into each. Season with black pepper, then bake for 10–15 minutes, until the egg whites are firm. Taste and season with a little more salt, if necessary. Top with a little gremolata and a sprinkling of sumac, and serve with bread.

# Eggs with ruby hollandaise & cavolo nero

*How to update classic eggs and hollandaise? Add a North African twist in the form of rose harissa (see page 29), which carries even the mildest foods to new heights. Here, it lends the hollandaise a beautiful, perfumed spice. If you don't want to make your own hollandaise, use a good-quality, shop-bought version and add the rose harissa to it.*

Serves 2

- 1 tbsp salt, for the cooking water
- vegetable or rapeseed oil
- 4 smoked streaky bacon rashers, diced
- 8 stems of cavolo nero, leaves picked and chopped
- 4 black garlic cloves, finely chopped
- 2 roasted red peppers from a jar, chopped
- 2 muffins, halved, or 4 slices of sourdough bread
- a dash of white wine vinegar
- 4 eggs

**FOR THE RUBY HOLLANDAISE**
- 100g unsalted butter
- 2 egg yolks
- 2 tsp rose harissa paste
- 1 lemon, zest and juice
- salt and black pepper

Fill a saucepan three quarters full of water, add the tablespoon of salt, place on a high heat and bring to the boil.

While the water is coming to the boil, place a frying pan on a medium–high heat and add a drizzle of oil. When hot, add the bacon pieces and fry for about 4–6 minutes, until golden and crispy, then add the cavolo nero, black garlic and red peppers. Sauté for 2–3 minutes, until the greens begin to soften and have taken on a little colour. Set aside and keep warm.

Make the ruby hollandaise. Lower the heat to bring the boiling water down to a simmer. Put the butter in a heatproof bowl and suspend the bowl in the pan, ensuring the bowl doesn't touch water. Stir the butter until melted. Take the bowl off the pan and allow the butter to cool slightly.

Whisk in the yolks, harissa and lemon zest and juice, season with salt and pepper and place the bowl back over the simmering water. Holding the bowl steady (protect your hands from the heat with a tea towel), whisk continuously for about 3–4 minutes, until the

hollandaise thickens slightly. Remove the bowl from the pan and set aside. Increase the heat to bring the water to the boil again.

Meanwhile, toast the muffin halves or sourdough to your liking.

Add the dash of white wine vinegar to the boiling water and give it a good stir. Then, while it's still moving, crack in the 4 eggs. Poach the eggs for 3–4 minutes, until the whites are firm and the yolks perfectly runny. Remove the eggs from the pan using a slotted spoon. (Alternatively, poach the eggs 2 at a time, leaving the first 2 to drain on kitchen paper while you cook the remaining eggs.)

Pile one quarter of the bacon mixture and an egg on top of each muffin half or slice of toast and finish with a spoonful of the ruby hollandaise. Serve immediately.

# Thai basil & galangal frittata

*Galangal is ginger's wild cousin – it's a little more fiery than common ginger root, but also a little sweeter. If you can't get hold of galangal paste, go ahead and use some ginger paste instead. Thai basil is more aromatic than regular basil, with a slight aniseed flavour. I like to have this dish as a really wake-you-up-in-the-morning sort of breakfast (it's satisfyingly filling), but it could equally make a good lunch or light supper served with a simple salad of lemon-dressed rocket.*

Serves 2–4

8 Thai basil leaves, chopped

2 garlic cloves, crushed

2 tsp galangal paste

6 eggs

50g parmesan, finely grated, plus extra to serve (optional)

a knob of unsalted butter

vegetable or rapeseed oil

100g new potatoes, cooked, then sliced into discs

1 spring onion, sliced

1 tsp Chilli Oil (see page 80)

salt

Put the basil leaves, garlic, and galangal paste in a mortar. Season with a little salt and pound the mixture with the pestle to a coarse paste.

In a bowl, beat the eggs with the parmesan, then mix in the basil mixture. Heat the grill to high.

Place a frying pan on a medium heat and add the butter and a drizzle of vegetable or rapeseed oil. When the butter has melted, add the cooked slices of potato and allow them to brown lightly on one side (about 5–7 minutes). Then, pour in the egg mixture, quickly stirring the eggs to incorporate the potatoes. Sprinkle over the spring onion and allow the mixture to cook

for about 3–4 minutes on a low–medium heat, until the frittata has set on the bottom. Place the pan under the grill for 5 minutes, until the top has browned and the frittata is almost set.

Drizzle the frittata with the chilli oil, sprinkle with a little more parmesan, if using, and serve in wedges straight from the pan. Or, turn out the frittata on to a warmed plate and then drizzle and sprinkle.

# Roasted cauliflower cheese

The ultimate expression of super-umami combined with flavourful ingredients that get the senses going, cauliflower cheese is also one of my favourite comfort foods. It's the multi-cheese and double-mustard combo in this recipe that makes it so powerful and so reassuring. Roasting your cauliflower before adding the cheese sauce gives a whole new dimension to this well-loved classic.

Serves 2–3

1 cauliflower, broken into florets

vegetable or rapeseed oil

50g unsalted butter

50g plain flour

500ml whole milk

100g vintage cheddar, grated

100g blue cheese, such as stilton, grated

1 tsp Dijon mustard

1 tsp wholegrain mustard

100g parmesan, grated

salt and freshly ground black pepper

Umami Crumbs (see page 132), to serve

Heat the oven to 220°C.

Place the cauliflower florets in a large ovenproof dish. Season well with salt and pepper and sprinkle over a generous glug of oil. Roast the cauliflower for about 15–20 minutes, until golden.

Meanwhile, place a saucepan on a medium heat, add the butter and allow to melt. Quickly whisk in the flour to form a completely smooth paste. Whisk to cook out the flour for 2 minutes, then gradually add the milk, whisking continuously. Add the cheddar, blue cheese and both mustards

and simmer on a low heat for 3 minutes to allow the cheeses to start to melt, then whisk on the heat until the cheeses are fully melted and combined. Set aside.

When the cauliflower is ready, remove it from the oven and sprinkle over half the parmesan. Place the cauliflower back in the oven for 5 minutes to crisp up, then remove and pour the cheese sauce over. Stir well, making sure all of the florets are coated, sprinkle the remaining parmesan over the top and put the cauliflower back in the oven again for 15 minutes, until the top is golden. Serve sprinkled with the umami crumbs.

**TASTE & FLAVOUR FACT**
In this recipe pre-cooking the cauliflower maintains bite to give some texture. The high temperature of the oil during roasting ensures that enzymes and carbohydrates interact to release aromas, brown the cauliflower and provide the desirable caramelised flavours.

# Roasted squash soup with porcini & miso

This soup has it all: it contains mushrooms and miso for the umami, yoghurt for the acidic lift and squash for a finishing touch of smooth sweetness. And, it's easy to make. If you haven't used miso before, this is an excellent starter recipe. Even though you need only a tablespoon of it here, miso keeps very well in the fridge and you can use it to add a savoury tang to gravies and other soups.

Serves 2

1 large butternut or onion squash

20g dried porcini mushrooms, rehydrated in 500ml hot water

1 tbsp dark miso

2 tsp Chilli Oil (see page 80)

1 tsp white pepper

vegetable or rapeseed oil

1 tbsp nigella seeds (optional)

**FOR THE MISO YOGHURT**

2 tbsp dark miso

5 tbsp full-fat yoghurt

Heat the oven to 180°C.

Place the whole squash on a baking tray and roast it for about 45 minutes, or until golden and soft (the precise roasting time will depend on the size of your squash). To test when it's cooked, push the skin with your thumb: if it gives slightly, it's ready.

Cut the cooked squash in half and discard the seeds. Scoop out the flesh either into a large blender, or into a bowl suitable for a hand-held stick blender. Slowly add the mushroom soaking water (not the mushrooms), blending between each addition, until you reach your preferred soup consistency. Add the dark miso, chilli oil and white pepper and set the soup aside to keep warm.

Place a large frying pan on a medium heat and add a drizzle of vegetable or rapeseed oil. When hot, fry the rehydrated porcini mushrooms for about 4–6 minutes, until super-dark and crispy on the outsides. Set aside.

Make the miso yoghurt by simply combining the ingredients in a bowl.

Ladle the soup into serving bowls. Swirl half the miso yoghurt into each bowl and top with the crispy mushrooms, and a sprinkle of the nigella seeds, if using.

Friends & Family

# Masala tomato soup
# with cheese & green chilli toasts

*This soup is everything you know and love about tomato soup, only better. The umami-rich tomatoes combined with a tumble of spices provide heightened flavour – but the ultimate experience for this recipe is in the cheddar and green chilli toasts, for dipping. Make the toasts from any bread you have to hand, or if you can find them, parathas (southeast Asian flatbreads) are superb.*

Serves 4

vegetable or rapeseed oil

1 large onion, chopped

4 garlic cloves, crushed, or 2 tsp garlic paste

2cm piece of ginger root, crushed or diced very small

a large pinch of salt

1 tsp ground coriander

1 tsp garam masala

1 tsp ground turmeric

1 tsp ground cumin

1 tsp medium curry powder

6 large tomatoes, roughly chopped

500ml vegetable stock

freshly ground black pepper

**FOR THE TOASTS**

30g vintage cheddar, grated

2 green chillies, finely chopped

4 slices of bread or 4 parathas

Place a large saucepan on a medium heat and add a generous glug of oil. When hot, add the onion and fry gently for a few minutes, until translucent. Add the garlic, ginger and salt, and cook, stirring occasionally for 3–4 minutes, until the garlic has taken on some colour. Put the lid on the pan (or use foil if you don't have a lid) and leave the onion and garlic mixture to sweat on a medium–high heat for 10–15 minutes, until completely softened and broken down.

Add the spices and fry, without the lid, for 1 minute or so, then add the tomatoes. Bring the mixture to a simmer and cook, without the lid, for 20 minutes. Then, add the stock and simmer again for another 20 minutes, until reduced by one third.

Transfer the mixture to a blender and blitz until silky. (Or, keep the soup in the pan and blend off the heat using a hand-held stick blender.) Keep warm.

Heat the grill to medium.

To make the toasts, combine the cheddar and chillies in a bowl and sprinkle the mixture liberally over the slices of bread or the parathas. Pop these under the grill for 4–5 minutes, until the cheese is melted and golden.

Ladle the soup into serving bowls, season with pepper, and serve the toasts alongside, cut into wedges.

Friends & Family

# Sprout & garam masala tart

*Sprouts sometimes get a bad rap, but turn them into crispy, aromatic, cheddary sprouts, then roast them in a tart and they will become a real treat. Mature, flavourful vintage cheddar provides the umami in this recipe. The cheesy sprouts alone, without the pastry, make an excellent side.*

Serves 2–4

1 large onion, roughly chopped

4 garlic cloves

½ red chilli

a generous pinch of salt, plus extra to season

vegetable or rapeseed oil

½ tsp garam masala

½ tsp ground turmeric

½ tsp ground coriander

12 Brussels sprouts, roughly sliced

2 tbsp double cream

1 tsp maple syrup

80g vintage cheddar, grated

1 x 320g sheet of ready-rolled puff pastry, at room temperature

1 egg, beaten

2 tsp nigella seeds

coriander leaves and chilli flakes, to serve

Heat the oven to 200°C. Blitz the onion, garlic, chilli and salt in a food processor to a paste.

Place a frying pan on a medium heat and add a drizzle of oil. When hot, add the paste and fry for 8 minutes, until soft, then reduce the heat and cover the pan (use foil if you don't have a lid). Allow the mixture to sweat for about 10 minutes, removing the lid and stirring occasionally to prevent burning. Add the garam masala, turmeric and ground coriander and cook, without the lid, for 1–2 minutes to cook out the spices (add 2 tablespoons of water to stop the paste catching, if needed).

Add the sliced sprouts to the pan and toss them in the paste. Fry for 4 minutes, then add a splash of water, along with the double cream, maple syrup and grated cheddar. Allow the cheddar a few moments to melt, then remove the pan from the heat and set aside.

Lay out the pastry sheet on a baking tray lined with baking paper (you can use the paper the pastry comes rolled in) and spoon the mixture on top, spreading it evenly, but leaving a 1–2cm border around the edge. Combine the beaten egg and the nigella seeds in a small bowl and use the mixture to brush the edges of the pastry.

Place the tart on the middle shelf of the oven and bake for about 20–25 minutes, until the pastry is crispy and the top is browned. Serve sprinkled with coriander leaves and chilli flakes.

# Quince & goat's cheese tart

*Quince jelly (traditionally and somewhat confusingly known as quince cheese) is the delicious jam made using the quince fruit, and is available from most supermarket delicatessen counters. It's an interesting way to add sweetness to a cheese tart (and, as a bonus fact, it also works brilliantly in gravies).*

Serves 4–6

olive oil

1 large onion, chopped

2 garlic cloves, crushed, or 1 tsp garlic paste

50g quince jelly

150g soft goat's cheese, plus extra to serve (optional)

a few thyme sprigs, leaves picked

a few rosemary sprigs, leaves picked

1 x 320g sheet of ready-rolled puff pastry, at room temperature

6 cherry tomatoes, halved

2 tsp nigella seeds

1 egg, beaten

freshly ground black pepper

a few mint leaves, shredded, to serve (optional)

Heat the oven to 180°C.

Place a frying pan on a medium–high heat and add a drizzle of oil. When hot, add the onion and fry for about 7–8 minutes, until deeply golden. Add the crushed garlic or the paste and fry gently for 1–2 minutes, then add the quince jelly, three quarters of the goat's cheese and the thyme and rosemary leaves. Leave to cook for 3–4 minutes, allowing the cheese to melt completely into the onion.

Lay out the pastry sheet on a baking tray lined with baking paper (you can use the paper the pastry comes rolled in) and spoon the mixture on top, spreading it evenly, but leaving a 1–2cm border around the edge. Scatter the cherry tomato halves over the top, crumble over the remaining goat's cheese, then sprinkle over the nigella seeds and season with pepper. Brush the edges with the beaten egg.

Place the tart on the middle shelf of the oven and bake for about 20–25 minutes, until the pastry is crispy and the top is browned. Serve sprinkled with shredded mint leaves and with a little extra goat's cheese crumbled over, if you like.

# Tomato tarte tatin

*For this twist on the French classic, I've paired tangy, umami-rich tomatoes with pomegranate molasses. The tarragon lends its aniseed notes, complementing the tomatoes' intensity. This recipe would also work well using any leftover pickled tomatoes from page 87. At Life Kitchen, we use a 23cm round cake tin to make the tatin, but any ovenproof dish that allows the pastry to fit snugly will do.*

Serves 2

2 tbsp pomegranate molasses

15 mixed-colour cherry tomatoes, halved

1 large vine tomato, cut into 4 thick slices

a few thyme or tarragon sprigs, leaves picked

1 x 320g sheet of ready-rolled puff pastry, at room temperature

20g parmesan, grated

salt and freshly ground black pepper

Heat the oven to 200°C.

Pour the pomegranate molasses into a 23cm solid-bottomed cake tin, or similar-sized ovenproof dish, then place the tomatoes, cut-sides downwards, on to it. Scatter the thyme or tarragon leaves over evenly and season well with salt and pepper.

Lay out the puff pastry sheet and, using the tin as a guide, trim it into a circle that it is just a bit larger than the circumference of the tin. Lay the puff pastry circle over the top of the tomatoes, neatly tucking in the edges. Prick the pastry with a fork (this will help it become nice and crisp) and

sprinkle with the parmesan. Place on the middle shelf of the oven and bake for 20–25 minutes, until the pastry is crispy and golden.

Remove the dish from the oven and place a serving platter over the top. Working quickly, hold the platter and flip to invert the tatin out on to it. Serve immediately.

Friends & Family

# Black & white couscous with roasted vegetables

*You can serve this recipe at a family feast or have it for two with plenty left over for lunch the following day. Balsamic vinegar, which is so often relegated to a drizzle on the plate, is perfect for adding flavour to plain couscous and works beautifully with lemon. The roasted vegetables add lots of natural sweetness to this dish.*

Serves 4–6

3 sweet potatoes, quartered or cut into large chunks

olive oil

2 red onions, quartered

a couple of thyme sprigs

a couple of rosemary sprigs

4 roasted red peppers from a jar, roughly sliced

6 spring onions

200g couscous

6 tbsp balsamic vinegar mixed into 150ml boiling water

1 vegetable stock cube dissolved in 150ml boiling water

75g sundried tomatoes (drained weight)

salt and freshly ground black pepper

1 tbsp za'atar, to serve

**FOR THE LEMON YOGHURT**

1 lemon, zest and juice, plus extra wedges to serve

4 tbsp full-fat Greek yoghurt

1 tbsp sundried tomato oil, from the jar

Heat the oven to 180°C.

Place the sweet potatoes on a baking tray, drizzle them with oil and give them a rub to coat. Season with salt and pepper, then roast for 25 minutes, until soft and lightly coloured.

Meanwhile, place the red onion quarters on a separate baking tray with the herbs. Drizzle with oil and season. Roast for 10 minutes, then add the peppers and spring onions to the tray and roast for a further 10 minutes, until everything is starting to colour.

While the vegetables are roasting, halve the couscous into separate bowls. Mix the balsamic and hot water mixture into one bowl; mix the vegetable stock into the other. (Make sure the water is boiling hot.) Cover both bowls with cling film, then leave to stand for 8–10 minutes, until the water is absorbed and the couscous is tender.

Fluff up both bowls of couscous with a fork and spoon them on to a serving platter or bowl (I like to spoon the white out first and add spoonfuls of the black). Add the sundried tomatoes on top.

When the vegetables are ready, scatter the roasted peppers and onions and the roasted sweet potatoes evenly over the top.

Make the lemon yoghurt. Mix all the ingredients together and add spoonfuls over the top of the platter.

Sprinkle over the za'atar for a final flourish and serve with lemon wedges alongside for squeezing over.

# Carbonara with mint & peas

We've been teaching this recipe at Life Kitchen since our very first class. Pancetta, parmesan and peas bring that sought-after umami hit, while mint leaves and chilli wake up the senses. And, of course, tagliatelle offers comfort that is so inherent in every bowl of lovely pasta. If you don't eat meat, crab (another provider of umami) is a worthy substitute.

Serves 4

**TASTE & FLAVOUR FACT**
Carbonara is a classic pasta dish, involving several sources of umami and many different textures. The addition of cooling mint, a trigeminal stimulant (see page 20), offers piquancy, making this version of carbonara especially good for those with a diminished sense of smell.

1 large onion, very roughly chopped

2 garlic cloves

1 red or green chilli, roughly chopped

vegetable or rapeseed oil

200g smoked bacon lardons

100g parmesan, grated, plus extra to serve

2 tsp salt, plus extra to season

4 eggs

400g dried tagliatelle

a large handful of frozen peas

a small handful of mint leaves, torn if large

freshly ground black pepper

Pulse the onion, garlic and chilli in a food processor to finely chop. (Or, finely chop by hand.)

Place a frying pan on a medium–low heat and add a glug of oil. When hot, add the chopped mixture and the lardons and season with salt. Cover with a lid (or use foil) and sweat on a low heat for 20–30 minutes, removing the lid to stir occasionally, until the onions have melted to a golden paste.

Meanwhile, beat together the grated parmesan and the eggs in a bowl and season with salt and pepper.

Bring a pan of water to the boil, add the 2 teaspoons of salt and cook the tagliatelle according to the packet instructions. Two minutes before the end of the cooking time, take 2 ladlefuls of the cooking water and stir it in to the parmesan and egg mixture.

Then, add the frozen peas to the pan with the pasta. When the pasta is cooked, drain it with the peas and tip everything back into the pan.

Add the parmesan and egg mixture and the onion and bacon mixture to the pasta and peas and stir – the sauce will take 2–3 minutes to heat through; just keep stirring and it will turn glossy and coat the pasta. Transfer to a serving dish and scatter over the mint leaves and extra parmesan.

# Cardamom & garam masala roasted lasagne

*Few things in life comfort me like a homemade lasagne. This one may be a continent away from the Italian classic, but what it lacks in familiarity, it makes up for in flavour – and ease. If you're short on time, you can use a good-quality, shop-bought béchamel, which you infuse with the cardamom and cheese – just remove the pods before you construct the lasagne. Serve with a leafy salad, or if you're Northern at heart, some chips.*

Serves 4–6

3 carrots, roughly chopped

1 celery stick, chopped

1 large onion, chopped

cloves of 1 garlic bulb

500g beef mince

½ tsp white pepper

½ tsp garam masala

½ tsp ground turmeric

¼ tsp freshly grated nutmeg

4 tbsp tomato purée

1 glass of red wine

2 x 400g tins of chopped tomatoes

12 dried lasagne sheets

a few slices of tomato (optional)

salt and black pepper

**FOR THE CARDAMOM BÉCHAMEL**

125g unsalted butter

10 cardamom pods, cracked

125g plain flour

500ml whole milk

50g parmesan or vintage cheddar, grated, plus extra for the topping

Heat the oven to 210°C.

Put the carrots, celery, onion and garlic in a food processor and pulse until everything is finely diced. (Or, just chop it all up as small as you can.)

In a large bowl, mix together the beef, chopped vegetables, spices and tomato purée. Spread the mixture in a single layer in a deep roasting tray and roast for about 30 minutes, until the mince is browned and a little bit crispy.

Add the red wine and tomatoes to the mince mixture, stir well, then return to the oven for a further 30 minutes, until reduced by half.

While the mince mixture is in the oven, make the cardamom béchamel. Place a saucepan on a medium–high heat, add the butter and allow to melt. Add the cracked cardamom pods.

Simmer on a low heat for 5 minutes to infuse, then remove the pods. Add the flour and whisk until smooth. Whisk to cook out the flour for 2 minutes, then slowly add all the milk, whisking continuously. Add the cheese and stir to stop it catching, until melted.

Now to assemble. Remove the beef and vegetables from the oven, taste and adjust the seasoning if needed. In a baking dish, add a thin layer of the cardamom béchamel, then a layer of lasagne sheets. Spoon over one third of the beef mixture, then top with lasagne. Repeat for the remaining thirds of the beef mixture, until you reach about 1cm from the top of your dish. Add the final layer of pasta and pour over the cardamom béchamel.

Grate over a good topping of parmesan or cheddar and top with a few sliced tomatoes, if using. Reduce the oven to 180°C and place the lasagne on the middle shelf. Bake for 45 minutes to 1 hour, until the top is golden and bubbling, the pasta is tender and the edges are crispy.

# Green risotto

*Risottos are so often said to be difficult, but they are nothing more than chopping, ladling and stirring. This type of cooking is about layering flavour. In this dish, the layers come from tangy fennel balanced out with sweet onion; silky and comforting butter and stock; and the pick-me-up of peas, chives and mint. It's a dish that leaves you both satisfied and wanting more.*

Serves 2–4

**FOR THE PEA PESTO**

150g frozen peas, defrosted

a handful of mint

1 green chilli, roughly chopped

1 lemon, zest and juice

50g parmesan, grated, plus extra shavings to serve

**FOR THE RISOTTO**

olive oil

1 fennel bulb, finely chopped

1 large onion, finely chopped

150g risotto rice

2 vegetable stock pots dissolved in 500ml boiling water

25g unsalted butter or 25ml olive oil

a large handful of chives, chopped

a large handful of mint leaves, chopped

salt

Put all the ingredients for the pea pesto in a food processor and blitz to a coarse paste (or put them in a bowl and use a hand-held stick blender). Set aside.

Make the risotto. Place a large saucepan on a medium heat and add a little oil. When hot, add the fennel and onion, and a sprinkling of salt to season. Sauté on a low heat for 10 minutes, until the vegetables are translucent (take care not to burn the onions). Add the risotto rice and stir well, then add the vegetable stock, a ladleful at a time, allowing the rice to absorb each addition before adding the next. Stir continuously – the whole process should take about 17 minutes. Finally, stir in the butter or olive oil, along with the chives and mint.

Stir the pea pesto into the risotto, then spoon into bowls and scatter with the parmesan shavings to serve.

# Green olive pasta

*This pasta went down a storm when we tested it at our tasting dinners for the book. Even those guests who thought they didn't like olives were surprised by the recipe's complex, umami flavours with a little bit of spice and a lemony zing at the end. Make this when you're in need of some hard-hitting flavour.*

Serves 4

2 tsp salt, plus extra to season

olive oil

1 onion, chopped

6 garlic cloves, crushed, or 3 tsp garlic paste

1 x 200g jar of pitted green olives in brine, drained and rinsed (gordal olives work very well)

½ red chilli, finely chopped (optional)

a few thyme sprigs, leaves picked

100g parmesan or vintage cheddar, grated, plus extra to serve

400g pasta of your choice (I like spirals or farfalle)

zest of 1 lemon

chilli flakes, to serve (optional)

Place a large saucepan of water on a high heat, add the 2 teaspoons of salt and bring to the boil.

Place a separate large saucepan on a medium heat and add a little oil. When hot, add the onion and fry for 5 minutes, until just golden. Add the garlic, fry for a few minutes, then add the olives, red chilli (if using) and thyme. Stir to combine, then transfer to a heatproof bowl. Using a hand-held stick blender, blitz to a smooth paste. Then, add the cheese and set aside to keep warm.

Once the water is boiling, cook the pasta according to the packet instructions. When cooked, reserve a mugful of the pasta water, then drain and return the pasta to the pan.

Stir the reserved pasta water a little at a time into the paste and, once you reach your desired consistency, spoon it over the cooked pasta. Stir, mix in the lemon zest and sprinkle with a grating of parmesan or cheddar, and some chilli flakes, if you like. Serve immediately.

# Currywurst traybake

*Originating in Germany, in its simplest form, currywurst is a sausage with curried ketchup. In this version I've boosted the umami-rich curried tomato sauce with smoked cheese – it's a quick and easy way to add savouriness to the dish. Serve this up with buttery mash when you're really in need of a comfort-food supper, or in a bap for a delicious, spiced sandwich.*

Serves 4

2 large onions, cut into 8 wedges

vegetable or rapeseed oil

75g unsalted butter

12 pork chipolatas

a large handful of kale, torn

200g tomato ketchup

1 x 400g tin of chopped tomatoes

6 tbsp roasted curry powder

2 tbsp smoked paprika

2 tbsp sherry vinegar

150g smoked cheese, broken into pieces

salt

Heat the oven to 180°C.

Place the onions in a deep baking tray, sprinkle over a little oil, season with a sprinkling of salt and turn to coat. Dot over the butter, then pop the tray in the oven for 25 minutes, until the onions are golden and caramelised. Stir the onions halfway through cooking to stop the edges from burning.

Once the onions are ready, add the sausages and kale to the tray and coat lightly in the juices. Put the tray back in the oven for 15 minutes, until the sausages are cooked through.

Meanwhile, make the sauce. Place a large saucepan on a medium heat and add all the remaining ingredients except the smoked cheese. Bring to a simmer and cook for 10 minutes, until reduced a little.

When the sausages are ready, remove the tray from the oven and coat the sausage mixture with the sauce (serve any extra sauce in a bowl alongside for spooning over). Scatter the pieces of smoked cheese over the top and pop the tray back in the oven to bake the currywurst for a further 10 minutes, until golden and bubbling.

Friends & Family

# Curried shepherd's pie with white pepper turnip mash

*Although this shepherd's pie has a few more spices than the traditional version I grew up with, it's not too far removed from that family favourite. The turnip mash adds an extra layer of flavour, particularly because I add lots of white pepper and butter, which – once you've tasted it – make it hard to go back to a standard mashed-potato topping. Of course, feel free to play with the spices to add your own twist.*

Serves 4–6

olive oil

500g beef mince

2 carrots, finely chopped

2 onions, finely chopped

6 garlic cloves, crushed, or 3 tsp garlic paste

½ tbsp ground turmeric

½ tbsp garam masala

½ tbsp ground cumin

½ tbsp ground coriander

2 tsp tomato purée

1 tbsp Marmite

a small glass of red wine (optional)

300ml beef stock

50g vintage cheddar, grated

buttered and minted peas, to serve

**FOR THE WHITE PEPPER TURNIP MASH**

1 large turnip, peeled and diced

a good pinch of salt

50g unsalted butter

1 tsp white pepper

Start the mash. Put the turnip in a saucepan with the salt and enough water to completely cover. Place the pan on a medium heat and bring the water to the boil. Then, reduce the heat and simmer for about 15–20 minutes, until the turnip is soft.

While the turnip is boiling, start the filling. Place a large saucepan on a high heat and add a glug of oil. When hot, add the beef, carrots and onions and fry for about 10 minutes, until the beef is browned. Drain off the rendered fat and leave the meat mixture on a high heat for 4–5 minutes, until it begins to caramelise. Add the garlic and fry, stirring to combine, for a couple of minutes, until the garlic is softened.

Add the spices and the tomato purée and Marmite. Stir well and allow the spices to cook out for 1 minute. Then, add the red wine, if using, and cook for a further 10 minutes to evaporate the alcohol (skip this step if you aren't using the wine). Add the beef stock and simmer for a further 30 minutes, or until the sauce has a thick, gravy-like consistency.

Meanwhile, heat the oven to 180°C.

Once the filling is reducing, the turnip should be nice and soft. Drain off the water and tip the turnip back into the pan with the butter and white pepper. Use a potato masher to make a nice, smooth mash. Set aside until the filling is ready.

Spoon the filling into an ovenproof dish, then top with the turnip mash. (If you like, you can pipe on the mash, but dolloped on is good enough.) Sprinkle the cheddar over and bake the shepherd's pie for 20 minutes, or until the top is golden. Serve with buttery minted peas.

# Paprika & shiitake fish pie

*Even if you're not a fan of fish pie, this recipe will win you over. It layers up the umami-rich foods (mushrooms, mackerel, peas, garlic, potato), while the smoked fish and paprika elevate it from humble family supper to a delicious feast worthy of serving up at an informal dinner party with friends. The tomato and basil mash on page 126 would be perfect as a topping, but store-bought mash is a great time saver.*

Serves 4–6

vegetable or rapeseed oil

1 large onion, sliced

a handful of shiitake mushrooms (or any mushrooms if you can't find shiitake), chopped

6 garlic cloves, chopped, or 3 tsp garlic paste

1 tsp smoked paprika

10 cherry tomatoes, halved

1 tbsp tomato purée (optional)

2 smoked mackerel fillets, broken into chunks

2 small skinless, boneless smoked haddock fillets (smoked basa or cod also works well), cut into chunks

150ml double cream

150g frozen peas

300g raw prawns, shelled

600g mashed potato

a small handful of chives, finely chopped

2 lemons, zest and juice

50g vintage cheddar, grated

salt and freshly ground black pepper

Heat the oven to 220°C.

Place a large saucepan on a high heat and add a glug of oil. When hot, add the onion and mushrooms and fry for 6–8 minutes, until the onion is deeply golden and caramelised. Add the garlic and fry for a further 2 minutes. Add the smoked paprika, cherry tomatoes and tomato purée (if using), along with 2 tablespoons of water to stop everything catching or burning.

Cook the mixture for 5 minutes, then add the chunks of fish to the pan, followed by the double cream, then the peas and prawns. Stir to combine, then remove the pan from the heat and transfer the mixture to an ovenproof dish.

Mix the mashed potato with the chives and the lemon zest and juice and season well.

Pipe or spread the mash over the fish filling, sprinkle the cheddar over and pop the fish pie in the oven to bake for 20 minutes, until the filling is bubbling, the smoked haddock and prawns are cooked through and the topping is golden.

**TASTE & FLAVOUR FACT**
Paprika is a bright-flavoured spice that adds plenty of aroma and stimulates the trigeminal nerve (see page 20) to create a gentle, warming sensation in the mouth.

# One-pot chicken & rice

*This is an easy, but impressive dish to serve at a family dinner. If you have time you can marinate the chicken overnight in the fridge to really get the flavour going – the yoghurt contains enzymes and acids that help break down the proteins in the meat to create chicken that's wonderfully tender and flavoursome. Serve it sprinkled with pomegranate seeds and fresh herbs, and flatbreads on the side.*

Serves 4–6

250g full-fat Greek yoghurt

1 tsp ground turmeric

1 tsp ground coriander

1 tsp garam masala

1 small chicken

3 cinnamon sticks (each about 4–6cm long)

1 large onion, chopped

vegetable or rapeseed oil

300g basmati rice

600ml hot chicken stock

1 tsp nigella seeds

1 tsp ginger paste

1 garlic clove, crushed

a handful of cashew nuts

a sprinkle of unsweetened desiccated coconut (optional)

salt and freshly ground black pepper

a handful of coriander leaves, to garnish

### FOR THE MINT YOGHURT

50g full-fat Greek yoghurt

2 tsp mint sauce

1 tsp caster sugar

Put the Greek yoghurt in a bowl and mix in the turmeric, coriander and garam masala. Season generously with salt and pepper, then rub the marinade all over the chicken to coat completely. At this point you can cover the coated chicken in cling film and place it in the fridge to marinate overnight, if you have time – or just go straight ahead and get cooking, as the spices will still give a wonderful flavour.

Place the cinnamon sticks inside the chicken and leave it, covered, on the side for about 1 hour, until it has come up to room temperature. Heat the oven to 210°C.

Put the chicken in a lidded casserole dish or deep roasting tray, place the chopped onion around the chicken and coat well with oil. Season with salt and pepper, then place the casserole or roasting tray, uncovered, on the middle shelf of the oven for 30 minutes.

Meanwhile, combine the ingredients for the mint yoghurt in a bowl, cover and pop it in the fridge until needed.

When the 30 minutes' cooking is almost up, reduce the oven to 180°C. Take out the casserole or tray and scatter the rice over the onion. Mix well, pour in the stock, add the nigella seeds, ginger and garlic and mix well again. Place the lid on the casserole, or cover the whole tray with foil so that no moisture can escape, and return the casserole or tray to the oven for 30 minutes. Then, remove the covering, sprinkle the cashews and the coconut (if using) on top of the rice mixture, and return to the oven again for a further 10 minutes, or until the rice is tender and the chicken is completely cooked through (so that the juices run clear).

Remove the casserole or tray from the oven, fluff up the rice and allow everything to rest for 20 minutes. Sprinkle with coriander leaves and serve with the mint yoghurt.

# Papaya bhuna

*This dish, a twist on the classic Bengali medium-spiced bhuna, is warming and comforting, with powerful spices. We've boosted its umami with tomatoes. The potatoes are optional – but, let's be honest, when are potatoes ever really an option?*

Serves 2–3

vegetable or rapeseed oil

1 large onion, chopped

1 tsp ginger paste, or 2cm piece of ginger root, peeled and grated

3 tsp garlic paste, or 6 cloves, crushed

½ green chilli, finely chopped (optional)

¼ tsp salt

2 tsp garam masala

1 tsp ground turmeric

1 tsp mild curry powder

2 large tomatoes, diced

1 large papaya, peeled and deseeded, then cut into large dice

1 large potato, chopped and boiled (optional)

**TO SERVE**

2 tsp nigella seeds

a few coriander leaves

warm, fluffy rice or flatbreads

Place a saucepan on a medium–high heat and add a generous glug of oil. When hot, add the onions and fry for 5–10 minutes, until browned. Add the ginger, garlic, chilli (if using) and salt, pop a lid on the pan (or use foil if you don't have a lid) and cook for about 15 minutes, to allow the mixture to completely sweat down and become soft.

Mix together the garam masala, turmeric and curry powder. Uncover the pan and add the spice mixture. Fry for 1–2 minutes to allow the spices to cook out – this is very important as it releases their flavour. Add 4 tablespoons of water, the tomatoes and papaya and allow everything to sweat down again, uncovered, for about 10 minutes on a medium heat. Add the potato, if using, bring the sauce to a simmer and cook, uncovered, for 10 minutes, until reduced and thick.

Sprinkle with the nigella seeds, scatter over the coriander leaves and serve immediately with rice or flatbreads.

# Cauliflower korma

*I love the aromatic sweetness of this curry. You can balance the flavours as you wish: if you really crave heat, add another chilli; if you don't, remove the chillies altogether. As it is, this recipe gives a little warmth, but not too much spice. Serve it with a classic mango chutney or the Green Chutney on page 134.*

Serves 2–4

- 3 tbsp unsweetened desiccated coconut
- 3 tbsp ground almonds
- 4 tsp garam masala
- 6 tbsp olive oil
- 1 whole cauliflower
- 6 garlic cloves, crushed, or 3 tsp garlic paste
- 1 large onion, chopped
- 2 tsp ginger paste, or 4cm piece of ginger root, peeled and grated
- 1 red chilli, roughly chopped
- 1 green chilli, roughly chopped
- a large pinch of salt, plus extra to season
- 1 tsp ground coriander
- 1 tsp ground turmeric
- 1 tsp ground cumin
- ¼ tsp white pepper
- ¼ tsp grated nutmeg
- 2 tbsp maple syrup
- 1 x 400g tin of full-fat coconut milk
- ½ vegetable stock cube or pot
- 400g spinach leaves
- 1 lemon, zest and juice
- freshly ground black pepper

**TO SERVE (OPTIONAL)**

- a handful of flaked almonds
- a few coriander leaves
- a handful of pomegranate seeds

Heat the oven to 220°C.

Place the desiccated coconut and ground almonds on a baking tray and roast for 5–6 minutes, until toasted. Remove and set aside.

Mix 3 teaspoons of the garam masala with 2 tablespoons of the olive oil. Season well and use to coat the cauliflower. Place the cauliflower on a baking tray and roast on the middle shelf of the oven for 30 minutes, until dark brown.

While the cauliflower is cooking, put the garlic, onion, ginger, chillies and the large pinch of salt in a food processor or blender and pulse to a rough paste. (Alternatively, put the ingredients in a bowl and use a hand-held stick blender.)

Place a saucepan on a medium heat and add the remaining olive oil. When hot, add the paste and cook for 4–6 minutes, stirring to make sure it doesn't catch or burn. Put a lid on the pan (or use foil if you don't have a lid) and simmer for 5–10 minutes to allow the aromas and flavours to intensify.

Combine the spices, then add them to the pan and stir. Cook, uncovered, for a few minutes, then add a dash of water.

Add the maple syrup, coconut milk, stock cube or pot, spinach leaves, lemon zest and juice and toasted coconut and almonds, then simmer on a high heat until the spinach wilts. You can serve the korma like this if you prefer, but I like to tip the whole lot into a food processor (or use a hand-held stick blender) and blend everything to a beautiful, green sauce.

When the cauliflower is ready, break it into florets and divide it between individual serving bowls. Spoon over the sauce and top with a sprinkling of almond flakes, coriander leaves and pomegranate seeds, if you like.

# Slow-cooked tamarind beef

*Tamarind, the fruit of the tamarind tree, is widely used in African and Asian cooking to provide an amazing tartness – one that in this recipe cuts through the richness of the beef. This dish is salty and deeply sumptuous, with an underlying sweetness from the umami-packed tomatoes.*

Serves 10

1.2kg beef brisket

3 tbsp vegetable or rapeseed oil

1 x 500g bag of soffritto mix (or 1 onion, 3 celery sticks, 1 large carrot and 4 garlic cloves, all chopped)

2 cinnamon sticks (each about 4–6cm long)

2 star anise

1 bird's eye chilli, finely chopped

3 tbsp ginger paste

3 tbsp tomato purée

2 beef stock cubes

6 tbsp tamarind concentrate

2 x 400g tins of chopped tomatoes

salt and freshly ground black pepper

**FOR THE MALTED CUCUMBER & CHILLI PICKLE**

½ cucumber, sliced into ribbons

1 large red chilli, sliced into very thin matchsticks

100ml malt vinegar

**TO SERVE**

6 soft white rolls, split in half

a handful of coriander leaves

Season the beef well with salt and pepper and allow it to come to room temperature (about 1 hour). Heat the oven to 220°C.

Place a large, ovenproof saucepan on a high heat and add the oil. When hot, add the beef and allow it to brown nicely on one side. After a few minutes, turn over the beef to brown on the other side and at the same time add the soffritto mix, cinnamon and star anise. Allow everything to cook for a few minutes, then add the remaining ingredients. Fill one of the tomato tins with water and add the water to the pan, too. Stir well.

Bring to the boil, then place the lid on the pan and pop it in the oven for 1 hour. Then, reduce the oven to 160°C and continue cooking the beef for

a further 1 hour. Remove the pan from the oven, turn the beef over and place it back in the oven to cook for a final 1 hour, until completely tender.

While the beef is cooking, make the malted cucumber and chilli pickle. Simply mix together the ingredients in a bowl. Set aside.

When the beef is ready, pull it apart with two forks, mixing the meat together with the sauce in the pot as you go. Generously pile equal amounts of the mixture on to the bottom halves of the buns, layer on the malted cucumber and chilli pickle, then add a flourish of coriander. Top with the bun lids and serve immediately.

**TASTE & FLAVOUR FACT**
Coriander divides people according to whether they like the taste or whether it tastes soapy and metallic. The difference is owing to a genetic variation in olfactory receptors between the two groups. If you're in the group that doesn't like coriander, simply leave it out.

# Pork & lemongrass skewers

*A well-known Vietnamese dish, these skewers are absolutely packed with intense flavour. They are also very satisfying to make – I think it's something about crafting the meat around the lemongrass stalks. The cucumber and mint dipping sauce works especially beautifully with this recipe, but it is something I could just as plentifully spoon over anything (especially jasmine rice) any night of the week.*

Makes 12 skewers

1 carrot, roughly chopped

½ leek, roughly chopped

6 spring onions, roughly chopped

2 tbsp garlic paste

2 tbsp ginger paste

1 tsp white pepper

1 red chilli, roughly chopped

1 green chilli, roughly chopped

a small handful of coriander

1 tsp caster sugar

500g pork mince

12 lemongrass stalks

vegetable or rapeseed oil

**FOR THE CUCUMBER & MINT DIPPING SAUCE**

¼ cucumber, peeled and diced

200ml rice vinegar

1 tbsp light soy sauce

1 tbsp caster sugar

1 tbsp chilli flakes, or ½ red chilli, finely chopped

10 mint leaves, sliced

Place all the skewer ingredients, except the pork, lemongrass stalks and oil, in a blender or food processor and blitz until smooth and incorporated. Add the pork and blitz again until the mixture forms a soft paste.

Taking equal amounts of the mixture each time, use your hands to shape it around the lemongrass stalks, starting about one third of the way up each stalk and moulding the mixture around until you reach the top, to form 12 skewers. Chill in the fridge for 10 minutes to firm up.

Place a large frying pan on a medium–high heat and add a good glug of oil. When hot, in batches, place the skewers in the pan, turning regularly until the meat is browned all over and cooked through (about 8–10 minutes per batch). Keep each batch warm in a low oven while you cook the next. (Alternatively, you can roast the skewers in an oven at 180°C for 20 minutes, until browned on the outsides and cooked through.)

To make the dipping sauce, simply combine all the ingredients in a small bowl. Serve alongside the skewers.

# Parmesan cod with salt & vinegar cucumber

*Think of British fish and chips with lashings of vinegar (with its acidic tang and sweetness), then turn up the flavour a few notches and you get this dish. Salt and vinegar cucumber is refreshing for your palate and the parmesan-crusted cod brings plenty of umami. Serve this with some crushed new potatoes.*

Serves 4

150g parmesan, grated

2 tsp smoked paprika

1 small handful of thyme, leaves picked

a pinch of salt

a pinch of black pepper

4 small cod loins (about 140g each)

2 eggs, lightly beaten

good-quality olive oil, to serve

**FOR THE SALT & VINEGAR CUCUMBER**

1 cucumber, sliced into ribbons

a large pinch of salt

150ml malt vinegar

Heat the oven to 180°C. Line a baking tray with baking paper.

Start the salt and vinegar cucumber. Place the cucumber ribbons in a bowl and sprinkle liberally with the salt, making sure all of the cucumber is salted – don't worry, you're going to wash off most of the salt later. Set aside.

To make the cod, in a bowl first mix the parmesan, paprika and thyme leaves with the pinches of salt and pepper.

One by one, place the cod loins into the beaten eggs and coat well. Then roll each egg-coated loin in the parmesan mixture until coated and place on the lined baking tray. Bake for about 8–10 minutes, until the cod gently flakes when pushed with the back of a teaspoon. If you like, give the loins a final minute under a hot grill to get the parmesan coating really crispy.

While the cod is in the oven, transfer the cucumber to a sieve and wash off the excess salt under running water. Place the ribbons in a bowl with the malt vinegar and give them a good mix. Leave to lightly pickle until the cod is cooked.

Serve each cod loin with a generous portion of the salt and vinegar cucumber and drizzled with good-quality olive oil.

# Chorizo lentils with Marmite cream cheese

*My friend Tom Cenci, a top London chef, has provided the inspiration for this recipe. Tom sweats down his onions for about five hours until they're rich, tangy and caramelised. While this recipe does not have quite the finesse or long cooking time of Tom's, it's comforting and homely.*

Serves 4

a small handful of pine nuts

½ tsp salt, plus extra to season

200g black or dark green lentils

150g unsalted butter

2 tbsp olive oil

3 large onions, sliced

200g chorizo, diced

500ml chicken stock

1 lemon, zest and juice

1 tbsp Marmite

90g full-fat cream cheese

freshly ground black pepper

a few chives or mint leaves, chopped, to garnish

First, toast the pine nuts. Place a frying pan on a medium heat. When hot, add the pine nuts and toast, moving constantly, for 2–4 minutes, until golden. Set aside.

Place a large saucepan of water on a high heat, add the ½ teaspoon of salt and bring to the boil. Add the lentils and boil for 20 minutes, until al dente. Drain and set aside.

While the lentils are cooking, place a frying pan on a low heat and add the butter and oil. When the butter has melted, add the onions and season with a sprinkling of salt. Sweat the onions for about 20–30 minutes, until they are golden and caramelised, but not dark.

Add the chorizo and fry gently for about 4–6 minutes, letting the chorizo release some of its oil. Add the al dente lentils and the stock, then bring the mixture to a simmer and cook for about 10 minutes, or until the lentils are fully cooked. Add the lemon zest and juice and season well with black pepper, and also a little salt if needed.

In a bowl, mix together the Marmite and cream cheese. Spoon dollops of the Marmite mixture on top of the lentils, then serve sprinkled with the toasted pine nuts and a few chopped chives or mint leaves.

# Savoy cabbage with pancetta

*The way the salty bacon in this recipe entangles with the rich cream creates for me the epitome of what comforting home cooking can be. You can add a clove or two of black garlic with the pancetta if you have it – but, truly, it's close to perfect as it is.*

Serves 2–4 as a snack

olive oil

150g diced smoked pancetta

1 savoy cabbage, thinly sliced

½ beef stock cube

50ml double cream

freshly ground black pepper

Place a large saucepan on a medium heat and add a small glug of oil. When hot, add the pancetta and fry for about 4–6 minutes, until golden.

Add the savoy cabbage to the pan, stir well to prevent the pancetta sticking, put a lid on the pan (or use foil if you don't have a lid) and cook for 3 minutes, until the cabbage begins to wilt. Then, crumble in the stock cube and stir in the double cream. Season with plenty of black pepper and cook for a few moments until the stock cube has dissolved and the cream begins to coat the cabbage. Remove from the heat and serve immediately.

**TASTE & FLAVOUR FACT**
In interactions between the basic tastes, salt reduces bitterness. In this recipe, the addition of slightly salty pancetta reduces the slightly bitter flavour in the savoy cabbage.

Friends & Family

# 'Nduja new potatoes with blue cheese

*'Nduja is a spicy, scarlet-coloured Italian pork paste and in this recipe it adds heat to the potatoes (it also makes a great condiment for a grilled cheese toastie). The powerful blue cheese is rounded off with the sweetness of the maple syrup and the aniseed freshness of the tarragon.*

Serves 2

2 tsp salt

a large handful of small new potatoes

2 tbsp 'nduja paste

a couple of tarragon sprigs, leaves picked

50g blue cheese (such as stilton), crumbled

maple syrup

1 lemon, zest and juice

Place a large saucepan of water on a high heat, add the salt and bring to the boil. Add the potatoes and boil for about 15–20 minutes, until soft. Drain the potatoes, lightly pressing them with the back of a spoon to burst them, then return to the pan and place them back on a medium heat.

Add the 'nduja and the tarragon leaves. Allow the spice to cook out for 2 minutes, then transfer the potatoes to a serving dish, crumble over the blue cheese, drizzle over some maple syrup and the lemon juice, and sprinkle over the zest. Serve immediately.

Friends & Family

# Sweets

# &

# Treats

During our research for this book, we repeatedly heard how our guests lose all desire to eat sweet things when they're going through treatment and recovery. This chapter is a little smaller than the others because of that, and we've kept its focus on the sour or tart end of the sweetness scale. The Lemon Posset Tart on page 202, for example, is reimagined in a pastry case (shop-bought for ease) that has been studded with sharp raspberries and then sprinkled with ruby-like pomegranate seeds designed to cut through any sugar.

For me, though, this chapter's stand-out recipe is the Miso White Chocolate & Frozen Berries on page 212. Inspired by the classic dessert on the menu at The Ivy in London, our version has the all-important umami twist: miso, a Life Kitchen favourite for its umami character, adds a delicate saltiness to the hot, white-chocolate sauce (think of the combination as the new salted caramel – and, remember, you heard it here first).

The first flavour hit for this chapter is the Raspberry & Rose Syrup on page 192. Perfumed and with a hint of sharpness, it takes only about 5 minutes to make and yet will liven up everything it touches. Some say it's magic, but I say it's actually just four wonderful ingredients working in harmony.

The second flavour hit is Sweet Cinnamon Dukkah on page 194. This is a sort of sweet seasoning – intended for sprinkling liberally over any dessert to add both pops of flavour and a boost for the flavours that are inherent in the dish. I particularly like it over the Lemon & Pomegranate Sherbet Cake on page 206, where it not only adds an additional layer of interest for the taste buds, but also provides instant texture and a sprinkling of delicate pink and green that adds beauty. However, don't feel limited – you can try it over pretty much any of the sweet treats in this chapter.

**Flavour hit**

# Raspberry & rose syrup

*Rose water is one of those magical ingredients that transforms a dish, but you have to be careful – it's a potent addition in cooking and in this case a little dash is all you need to turn your raspberries into something sweet and floral. The resulting perfumed tartness will enhance just about anything. Store the syrup in a sterilised jar in the fridge for up to 1 week.*

Makes 200ml

200g raspberries

½–1 tsp rose water, to taste

2 tbsp maple syrup

½ lemon, zest and juice

Place a saucepan on a medium heat and add all the ingredients. Bring the liquid to a simmer and cook for about 5 minutes, until the raspberries break down slightly. Remove the pan from the heat and allow the mixture to cool. If you like your syrup smooth, strain the mixture through a sieve into a sterilised jar – but I like it chunky, so I just store it as it is.

*Especially good for drizzling over...*
Lemon Posset Tart (see page 202)
Baked Berries with Pomegranate Meringue (see page 205)
Lemon & Pomegranate Sherbet Cake (see page 206)
Paddington Pudding (see page 208)

**TASTE & FLAVOUR FACT**
Combining fruit and floral aromas can produce powerful flavour combinations (we often experience these when we drink red wine). The intense flavour of raspberry comes, in particular, from ketone molecules that make an especially harmonious match for the floral notes in rose water, which is why this syrup is such a flavour hit.

# Sweet cinnamon dukkah

*Dukkah is an Egyptian spice mixture usually reserved for savoury dishes. For this book, though, I've given it a sweet spin. Rose is a really great ingredient for stimulating your palate as it engages your sense of smell. Cinnamon wakes up the trigeminal nerve to really heighten the sensations in your mouth. Serving suggestions are below, but for me it suits any and every sweet dish. Store in an airtight container in a cool, dark place for 2–3 months.*

Makes about 200g

50g shelled pistachios

150g hazelnuts

50g white sesame seeds

4 cardamom pods

3 tbsp ground cinnamon

1 tbsp edible dried rose petals

Heat the oven to 190°C.

Put the pistachios and hazelnuts on one baking tray and the sesame seeds on another. Roast the nuts for 8–10 minutes and the sesame seeds for 6–8 minutes, until golden. Remove from the oven and allow to cool slightly (the cooling is important, because if the nuts and seeds are too hot when you blend them, they may turn into nut or seed butter).

Use a knife to split open the cardamom pods and remove the black seeds inside. Discard the pods.

Once the roasted nuts and seeds have cooled, tip them into a food processor or blender with the cardamom seeds and all the remaining ingredients and pulse until roughly chopped.

*Especially good for sprinkling over...*
Baked Yoghurt with Rose (see page 196)
Peach Galette with Citrus Cream (see page 200)
Lemon & Pomegranate Sherbet Cake (see page 206)
Paddington Pudding (see page 208)

# Baked yoghurt with rose

*Baked yoghurt is a traditional, creamy Bengali dessert. This version is laced with fragrant rose water and is smooth and refreshing enough to pass not just as a dessert, but as a breakfast, too. This recipe includes an intensely zesty and sweet orange syrup, but you could use Raspberry & Rose Syrup (see page 192), if you prefer. A sprinkling of roasted pistachios adds texture, although grated chocolate would also be really tasty.*

Serves 6

250g condensed milk

250g full-fat Greek yoghurt

1 lemon, zest and juice

1–2 tsp rose water, to taste

**FOR THE ORANGE SYRUP**

1 orange, zest and juice

2 tbsp light brown soft sugar

**TO SERVE**

a small handful of roasted pistachios (see page 194), chopped

a small handful of edible dried rose petals (optional)

Heat the oven to 150°C.

Put all the ingredients except the serving ingredients in a large bowl (use more or less rose water, depending on strength), then whisk to combine. Pour equally into six ovenproof ramekins or brûlée dishes.

Set the ramekins or dishes on a baking tray and bake on the middle shelf of the oven for 20 minutes, until firm but not totally set.

Meanwhile, make the orange syrup. Place the zest, juice and sugar in a small pan on a medium heat and simmer for 10 minutes, until the sugar has dissolved and the mixture thickened. Set aside.

When the baked yoghurts are ready, remove them from the oven. Eat warm; or, leave to cool, then pop them in the fridge to chill and eat cold. Either way, before serving, drizzle with the syrup and sprinkle over some chopped, roasted pistachios, and a few dried rose petals, if you like.

# Tiramisu's cousin

*To add extra tang and acidity, I've swapped out mascarpone for Greek yoghurt in this version of the Italian classic tiramisu. Tart cherries bring a touch of vibrancy. This dessert is really easy to make – you can pull it together in 15 minutes and it will keep in the fridge for a few days.*

Serves 8

1 x 200g packet of sponge fingers

**FOR THE CHERRY-COFFEE MIXTURE**

4 tbsp caster sugar

150ml good-quality coffee

1 x 425g tin of black cherries in syrup, drained and pitted, plus extra to decorate

**FOR THE CREAM**

300ml double cream

300ml full-fat Greek yoghurt

1 lemon, zest and juice

2 small oranges, zest and juice, plus extra zest to decorate (optional)

4 tbsp caster sugar

Make the cherry-coffee mixture. Stir the sugar into the coffee, then blitz it with the cherries in a food processor or blender. (Or, crush it all with a fork.)

Put all the cream ingredients in a bowl and whip to soft peaks.

Line individual serving dishes with the sponge fingers and pour over equal amounts of the cherry-coffee mixture, then the cream. Repeat once or twice more to create layers. Dot with extra cherries, then chill in the fridge for 1 hour, until set. Sprinkle with extra zest to decorate, if you like.

# Peach galette with citrus cream

*Peaches and cream are best friends, and the floral, decadent orange blossom water really adds something magical to this dessert. You can add the leftover peach juice to iced black tea for a quick-and-easy refreshing drink, if you like.*

Serves 6–8

1 x 400g tin of peach slices in juice, drained

100g caster sugar

½ tbsp vanilla bean paste or extract

1 orange, zest and juice

1–2 tsp orange blossom water, to taste

1 x 320g sheet of ready-rolled shortcrust pastry, at room temperature

1 egg, lightly beaten

a few chopped pistachios, to serve

**FOR THE CITRUS CREAM**

200ml double cream

2 tbsp golden caster sugar or caster sugar

1 lime, zest and juice

Heat the oven to 180°C.

Place the peach slices in a bowl. Add the sugar, vanilla, orange zest and juice and orange blossom water and stir to combine, making sure all of the peach slices are well coated.

Line a baking sheet with baking paper (you can use the paper the pastry comes rolled in) and lay out the pastry on top. Place the peach slices in the middle, in any way you please, and bring the edges of the pastry towards the middle to create a rough circle – you can trim to round off the pastry where the corners were, if you like, but don't worry about being too neat.

Using a pastry brush, lightly glaze the pastry edges with the beaten egg. If you prefer the look of a dark glaze, you can put the galette in the freezer for 5 minutes and then give it a second egg glaze.

Bake the galette for 30–40 minutes, or until the pastry is crisp and golden and the peaches are glistening.

While the galette is in the oven, make the citrus cream. Whip the cream together with the sugar and lime zest and juice (keep a little zest to serve) until it forms soft peaks. Transfer to a serving dish and pop it in the fridge until you're ready to serve the galette.

Once the galette is ready, sprinkle the pistachios over the top, and sprinkle the reserved lime zest into the bowl of citrus cream. Serve the galette warm with the cream alongside for dolloping.

Sweets & Treats

# Lemon posset tart

*For me, a simple posset is the best dessert: the sweetness balanced with the bright citrus is a pairing that sings in harmony. However, Life Kitchen research has shown me that desserts need a high ratio of tang to sweetness to be really impactful, so I've added pomegranate in this recipe to increase the tartness. If you prefer not to put the filling in a pastry case, pour it into glasses or ramekins to make individual possets.*

Serves 6–8

500ml double cream

200g golden caster sugar

2 limes, zest and juice

2 lemons, zest and juice

a small handful of raspberries

a small handful of pomegranate seeds

1 shop-bought 23cm pastry case

pomegranate molasses or Raspberry & Rose Syrup (see page 192), to serve (optional)

Place a large saucepan on a medium heat and add the cream, sugar and zest and juice of both citrus fruits. Stir gently for about 2–3 minutes, until the sugar dissolves. Then, bring the mixture to a very gentle boil for 3–5 minutes, until thickened. Remove from the heat and set aside to cool slightly.

Sprinkle most of the raspberries and pomegranate seeds evenly across the tart base and pour over the citrus cream mixture.

Put the tart in the fridge to set for 3–4 hours. When set, sprinkle over the remaining pomegranate seeds and raspberries, then drizzle over some pomegranate molasses or raspberry and rose syrup, if you like.

**TASTE & FLAVOUR FACT**
Lemons add a darting 'lift' to a dish, because the sour receptors on our tongue fire up more quickly than the sweet, savoury or bitter receptors.

# Baked berries with pomegranate meringue

*One of the things that makes this dessert so fantastic is how gorgeous it looks, yet how easy it is to throw together. The orange and berries are fruity and bright with a little bit of sweetness from the pomegranate-studded meringue.*

Serves 4–6

2 large handfuls of mixed berries

1 orange, zest and juice

2 tbsp pomegranate molasses

2 egg whites

100g golden caster sugar

2 tbsp pomegranate seeds

Heat the oven to 150°C.

In an ovenproof dish, mix together the berries with the orange juice and zest and the pomegranate molasses.

Put the egg whites in a bowl and, using an electric hand whisk, whisk the egg whites to soft peaks. Add the sugar, 1 tablespoon at a time, whisking between each addition, until the sugar is incorporated and you have firm, glossy peaks. Gently fold in the pomegranate seeds until evenly distributed.

Spoon the meringue on top of the berries and place the dish on the middle shelf of the oven for 15–20 minutes, until the meringue is golden on the outside, but soft in the middle. Serve warm.

# Lemon & pomegranate sherbet cake

*This is a cake made in an unusual way. By combining everything in a pan, there's no need to beat the butter and sugar together first, as is more conventional in cake-making. The tartly sweet pomegranate and lemon combination gives this cake its sherbet tang. If you have the energy to make the icing, the cake will be pretty as a picture (however, it's equally as scrumptious without).*

Serves 8–10

250g unsalted butter

250g golden caster sugar

3 lemons, zest and juice

250g self-raising flour, sifted

4 eggs

a large handful of pomegranate seeds, plus 1 tbsp to decorate

a few chopped pistachios or a sprinkling of Sweet Cinnamon Dukkah (see page 194), to decorate

a few mint leaves, to decorate

**FOR THE GLAZE**

3 tbsp pomegranate molasses

1 tbsp maple syrup

1 lemon, zest and juice

**FOR THE ICING (OPTIONAL)**

100g icing sugar

4 tbsp pomegranate molasses

Heat the oven to 180°C. Grease a 23cm loose-bottomed cake tin with butter.

Place a large saucepan on a medium heat and add the butter, sugar and lemon zest and juice. Allow the butter and sugar to melt together, then add all the flour and whisk quickly to incorporate.

Remove the pan from the heat and, one at a time, beat in the eggs, then stir in the large handful of pomegranate seeds.

Transfer the mixture to the cake tin, level the top and bake for about 35 minutes, until the crust is golden and crunchy and a skewer inserted into the centre comes out clean. (Bake a little longer if the cake needs it.)

While the cake is baking, make the glaze. Mix together the pomegranate molasses, maple syrup and lemon zest and juice. Set aside.

Once the cake is ready, pour the glaze over the top while the cake is still hot. Then, leave to cool completely in the tin.

If you're making the icing, mix together the icing sugar and the pomegranate molasses in a bowl. Add a couple of teaspoons of water to loosen, if necessary – although, the icing should be nice and thick.

Remove the cake from the tin, and, if using, drizzle the icing over. Decorate with the remaining pomegranate seeds, the pistachios or sweet cinnamon dukkah and the mint leaves.

Sweets & Treats

# Paddington pudding

*The Life Kitchen classes have taught me so much about my guests' favourite things to eat when living with cancer. Something that comes up a lot is marmalade. This is my marmalade-y take on a bread-and-butter pudding.*

Serves 6

6 croissants, halved lengthways

3 tbsp unsalted butter

8 tbsp orange marmalade

250g vanilla custard

10 cardamom pods, cracked

4 tbsp caster sugar

1 lemon, zest and juice

Heat the oven to 180°C.

Open out the halved croissants and butter the bottom halves, then slather on the marmalade. Replace the tops and tuck the croissants into an ovenproof dish so that they fit snugly.

Place a saucepan on a medium heat, add the custard and cracked cardamom pods and bring to a gentle boil to help the flavour to infuse. Remove the pan from the heat and leave the custard to cool slightly, then pour it through a sieve over the croissants, discarding the cardamom pods.

Bake the pudding on the middle shelf of the oven for 30 minutes, until the top is browned.

Mix together the sugar and the lemon zest and juice and sprinkle the mixture over the pudding. Return the pudding to the oven for 5 minutes to glaze, then serve.

Sweets & Treats

# Roasted watermelon granita

*Although watermelon itself has a mild flavour, pair it with chilli and lime and it gains almost tomato-like intensity. I've roasted it here, which really helps it to absorb the other flavours to give you something deeply refreshing. Make the granita when you have some time, then it will be ready to pull out of the freezer whenever you need to feel cooled and refreshed.*

Serves 3–5

½ small watermelon, deseeded, or 400g read-to-eat diced watermelon

1 green or red chilli, chopped

2 limes, zest and juice, plus extra zest to serve

2 tbsp light brown soft sugar

Heat the oven to 180°C.

If you're using half a watermelon, scoop out the flesh and cut it into 2cm dice (eat a couple of bits, just for good measure).

Place the dice on a baking tray. In a small bowl, mix together the chilli, lime juice and sugar and pour this over the watermelon, tossing to coat. Sprinkle over the lime zest, then roast for 25 minutes, until the sugar and lime caramelise.

Leave the roasted watermelon to cool, then transfer it to a freezer bag and freeze for 4 hours. Then, pop it in a food processor or blender and whizz it until you have a smooth and icy consistency.

Serve immediately, sprinkled with a little extra lime zest, or transfer the granita to a freezer-proof container and pop it back in the freezer for tucking into whenever you need it.

# Miso white chocolate & frozen berries

*Miso is the magic in this dessert, because its saltiness perfectly balances out the sweetness of the white chocolate – rather in the way that salted caramel works. Not only is the miso-white chocolate combo completely delicious, it's also incredibly easy to throw together. The hot and cold nature of this dish is both surprising and soothing.*

Serves 4–6

300ml double cream

300g white chocolate, broken into pieces

1 tbsp white miso

1 x 300g bag of frozen berries, slightly thawed

Place a saucepan on a low heat and add the double cream and white chocolate. Allow the chocolate to melt, making sure it doesn't stick to the bottom of the pan. Once it has melted, quickly whisk in the miso until it's fully incorporated, trying not to leave any lumps.

Place your frozen berries in a serving dish and pour over a little of the hot chocolate and miso mixture. Allow the berries to soften for a few moments, then pour over the remaining sauce. Serve immediately.

**TASTE & FLAVOUR FACT**
Adding umami-rich miso to white chocolate's sweet cocoa butter creates a sweet–salt–savoury balance that is the key to this dessert's intense and satisfying flavour.

# Index

# Cook's notes

I used a standard fan oven for all of my recipes, so have given fan temperatures in the book. If you're using a conventional oven, increase the stated temperature by 20°C as a rule of thumb.

Sterilise clean jars and lids by running them through the dishwasher on a hot cycle and leaving them to dry before removing. Or, 'bake' them in an oven at 180°C for 15 minutes.

I use sea salt when seasoning all ingredients and table salt in water for boiling pasta, potatoes and so on. Extra-virgin olive oil is great for using raw in salads and dressings, but standard olive oil is fine for use in cooking. Use fresh herbs and medium-sized eggs, unless otherwise stated.

Always buy the best ingredients you can afford, but don't get hung up on this and remember to have fun with food!

Finally, if you have low immunity, take care with ingredients such as shellfish and raw or undercooked eggs. Consult your doctor if you are unsure as to the suitability of any recipe.

# Acknowledgements

Thanks to my wonderful family: Dad, Rachael and Sarah, my nana, aunties, uncles, cousins and family friends who have believed in Life Kitchen from the start. To my friends, especially Kim and Racheal, without whom I would not have managed to get the project going. To Oliver, whose love, support and guidance have helped shaped my career – and my life.

To Hugh Fearnley-Whittingstall, for guiding our first steps and for offering River Cottage as the venue for our inaugural Life Kitchen class; to Nigella Lawson, for her early support and her continuing advice and for being such a fabulous icon; to Mitzie Wilson for her early belief in me and huge encouragement; and to Barry Smith for being such an integral part of the science that has made Life Kitchen what it is today.

To Bloomsbury's team: Richard for seeing my vision and commissioning this book; Natalie for the perfect way in which she has guided it into reality; Kitty and Jude for keeping us on track and for sensitive attention to detail; Lawrence for his beautiful typography and design; and Thi, Ellen and Don for being the best publicity and marketing team.

To Clare Winfield for being the best photographer in the business; Polly Webb-Wilson for beautiful styling; and Lara Harwood for her stunning illustrations and for executing my vision through colour and motion.

To Debora Robertson for being an adviser and a friend and for letting me use her house for shooting some of the best images in the book. And to Kevin Gibson for additional photography and for bringing the Life Kitchen Cookery School to life through his images.

To my agents, Claudia Young at Greene & Heaton and Felicity Blunt at Curtis Brown, for helping me to navigate the worlds of publishing and the media.

To the cookery schools, festivals, NHS trusts and charities who have hosted us, helped us and been a significant part of the Life Kitchen journey. And to all of our incredibly generous Life Kitchen supporters, without whom none of this would have been possible.

And, lastly, to our guests – the heroes of this story. Thank you.

# Life Kitchen at the Lodge

Since we started Life Kitchen, Kimberley and I have travelled all over the country offering pop-up cookery classes. From River Cottage in Dorset to restaurants in Blackfriars in London, Newcastle and Manchester and (thanks to help from Maggie's Cancer Centres) many more in between, Life Kitchen has reached hundreds of people living with cancer. In 2019, as well as being out on the road, I wanted to open a school in a permanent location. For me, the only place that could be was in Sunderland, my home town and the place that would most fittingly honour my mother's memory. I approached our local council for support. They launched into action, offering me a choice of ten possible sites – one of which was the Grade II-listed gate lodge on the edge of Mowbray Park. The stunning Victorian exterior belied an unloved, stark office interior – but the space had potential, and the views from the windows, over the park, were simply gorgeous.

Work began to realise my vision to create a permanent cookery school where our guests could feel completely at home. We've had incredibly generous support from local and national businesses, who donated both time and resources to make this vision a reality. It's no exaggeration to say that we couldn't have done it without them and we are grateful to every one.

Life Kitchen at the Lodge opened its doors in summer 2019. It is now a bright, light and inviting space – like the most beautiful home kitchen. The views from the central cookery island look out over the park. Our school can accommodate up to ten guests at a time – that space, which at first might have seemed too small to be practical, means that every session feels incredibly connected, and that's just how I wanted it.

My inaugural class at the Lodge will always be particularly special, of course. Our first ten guests brought with them a fundamental energy and positivity that made the atmosphere wholly magical. That magic is something we aim to capture every time we welcome people to Life Kitchen at the Lodge. I still can't quite believe that the school is there – breathing fresh life into a building that has existed for hundreds of years and belonging just as much to the community as it belongs to me.

BLOOMSBURY PUBLISHING
Bloomsbury Publishing Plc
50 Bedford Square, London, WC1B 3DP, UK

BLOOMSBURY, BLOOMSBURY PUBLISHING and the Diana logo are trademarks of
Bloomsbury Publishing Plc.

First published in Great Britain 2020

A catalogue record for this book is available from the British Library.

ISBN: HB: 978-1-5266-1229-8; eBook: 978-1-5266-1222-9

2 4 6 8 10 9 7 5 3 1

*Designer:* Lawrence Morton
*Project Editor:* Judy Barratt
*Photographer:* Clare Winfield
*Illustrator:* Lara Harwood

*Food Stylists:* Ryan Riley and
Kimberley Duke
*Prop Stylist:* Polly Webb-Wilson

Printed and bound in China by C&C Offset Printing Co. Ltd.

Bloomsbury Publishing Plc makes every effort to ensure that the papers used in the manufacture of our books
are natural, recyclable products made from wood grown in well-managed forests.
Our manufacturing processes conform to the environmental regulations of the country of origin.

To find out more about our authors and books visit www.bloomsbury.com and
sign up for our newsletters.